Table of Contents

List of Figures

List of Tables

Speech Recognition Using the

Mellin Transform

I.   Introduction

Speech recognition has many military and commercial applications, for example: hands-free voice control of cockpit or automotive controls; voice-based data entry for applications that would normally require several mouse clicks or have several text entry fields; telephony applications such as telephone banking, catalogue centers, and call routing for customer service centers; and voice-based biometrics, etc. Because of the wide applicability of speech recognition, it has received a great deal of research for a number of decades [1]. Despite this considerable attention, automatic speech recognizers still do not perform as well as human for most tasks.

One problem in speech recognition is achieving good speaker-independent performance. A speech recognizer trained on many examples of speech for a given individual can often perform well. However, a recognizer trained on the same amount of data but from a wide range of speakers, usually does not perform nearly as well. There are a number of reasons why this is the case. For example, women and children tend to have shorter vocal tracts than men, leading to shifts in the formants (vocal tract resonances). Also, women and children tend to have higher average pitch than men. Another reason is the different accents and dialects among speakers. These various differences among speakers cause considerable variability in the standard features used in speech recognition, which in turn reduces the phoneme discrimination of a recognizer, where phonemes are basic elements of speech. This research attempts to partially address

1

this speaker-independent speech recognition problem through the use of a feature set based on an auditory model and the Mellin transform.

The Mellin transform (MT) [2] is the integral transform

$$M_{f(t)}(s) = \int_0^{\infty} t^{s-1} f(t) \, dt, \quad s \in \mathbb{C}.$$

(1)

The usefulness of the MT lies in its scaling property. Research has shown that the MT normalizes vowel feature sets from speakers with different voice pitches [3]. The benefits of the MT with an auditory model are that it helps to separate pitch information from the vocal tract configuration and that it generates a representation that separates the vocal tract size information from the general shape information. The research conducted here uses an entirely new approach in the field of speech recognition by performing the MT on all speech data, not just vowels, to determine if features from the MT lead to improved phoneme discrimination across speakers.

For this research several Matlab scripts were written to run experiments and to supplement previously written code. Altering part of the code that executes the MT resulted in a reduction in computation time by a factor of four. Hidden Markov models (HMMs) were used to perform recognition experiments. The results were compared to results from traditional automatic speech recognition (ASR) using the standard features, which are mel frequency cepstral coefficients (MFCCs). The results obtained from the speech recognition experiments show a recognition rate improvement for some phonemes over conventional methods used in ASR.

Chapter 2 discusses the terms and the basic tools used in this research and provides a background for understanding the methodology. Chapter 3 discusses the experimental methodology, including steps for obtaining results and why each step was taken. Chapter 4 analyzes the results, and Chapter 5 provides a discussion and recommendations for future research.

II.   Background

This chapter discusses the basics of speech recognition and also defines the terms and tools used to accomplish the results of this research.   Once a background understanding of the methods for speech recognition is reached, the experimental methodology discussed in Chapter 3 will be understood more completely.

2.1 Speech Recognition Basics

As mentioned in the previous chapter, speech recognition is highly challenging in that it requires developing statistical models to understand and recognize human speech. The basic model for a speech recognition system is shown in Figure 1. The first step is to extract features from the speech that will be used in the pattern recognition analysis to recognize the speech. Successful speech recognition requires prior knowledge in the form of an acoustic model, a pronunciation dictionary, and a language model. The recognizer uses the prior knowledge sources and the feature vectors to determine a set of words according to the fundamental speech recognition equation [4] given as:

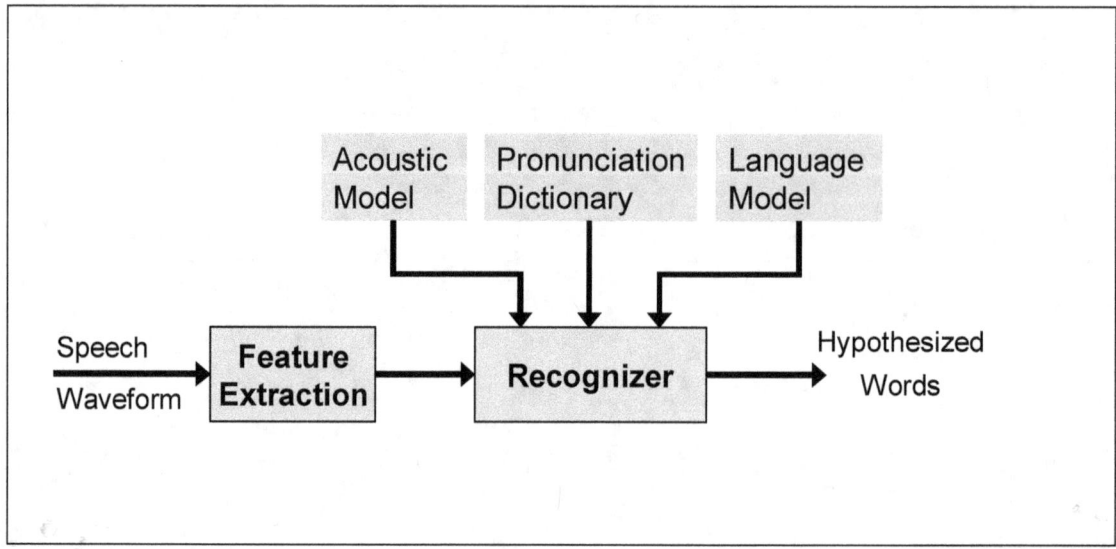

Figure 1. A block diagram of the basic model for speech recognition.

$$\underline{w}' = \arg \max_{\underline{w}} P\left(\underline{w} \mid X\right). \tag{2}$$

This equation states that the hypothesized words, $\underline{w}'$, equal the argument that maximizes the probability of the words, $\underline{w}$, given the acoustical features matrix X. Using Bayes' rule, this equation becomes

$$\underline{w}' = \arg \max_{\underline{w}} \frac{P\left(X \mid \underline{w}\right) P\left(\underline{w}\right)}{P\left(X\right)}. \tag{3}$$

The probability P($\underline{X}$) of the feature matrix is simply a scalar constant for all word sequences, so it can be ignored. This leaves the following equation to describe the speech recognition process:

$$\underline{w}' = \arg \max_{\underline{w}} P\left(X \mid \underline{w}\right) P\left(\underline{w}\right) \tag{4}$$

The P($\underline{w}$) term is the prior probability of a sequence of words, $\underline{w}$, which is described by the language model. Language models are one component that a speech recognizer uses and are discussed in further detail below in Section 2.2. The P($X|\underline{w}$) factor is the probability of a feature matrix given the word sequence, $\underline{w}$. This term is taken into account through the acoustic models.

The final component for a speech recognizer is a pronunciation dictionary. An example of part of a pronunciation dictionary is shown in Table 1. The pronunciation dictionary tells the recognizer how words are broken up into smaller units called phonemes, which are the smallest basic units of speech. There are about 39 different phonemes in the English language. Speech recognition is often performed using phoneme-level acoustic models rather than word-level models. This is due to a lack of data necessary for training individual word models. This research uses phoneme-level acoustic models.

ABBREVIATE	[ABBREVIATE]	AH B R IY V IY EY T SP
ABBREVIATE	[ABBREVIATE]	AX B R IY V IY EY T SP
ABDOMEN	[ABDOMEN]	AE B D OW M AH N SP
ABDOMEN	[ABDOMEN]	AE B D AX M AX N SP
ABIDES	[ABIDES]	AH B AY D Z SP
ABIDES	[ABIDES]	AX B AY D Z SP
ABILITY	[ABILITY]	AH B IH L AH T IY SP
ABILITY	[ABILITY]	AX B IH L IX T IY SP
ABLE	[ABLE]	EY B AH L SP
ABLE	[ABLE]	EY B EL SP

Table 1. Part of a typical pronunciation dictionary used for speech recognition. The first column is the word to be recognized, the second column is the output when that word is recognized, and the third column shows a breakdown of all the phonemes that make up each word, where "SP" denotes a short pause.

2.2 Language Models

Language models estimate the probability of sequences of words [4]. A speech recognizer uses a language model to estimate the probability a given word will follow another word in a spoken sequence. Common language models are bigram and trigram models. These models contain computed probabilities of groupings of two or three particular words in a sequence, respectively. This project uses a phoneme-level language model for phoneme recognition experiments. The phoneme-level language model used in this research, allows any phoneme to follow any other phoneme with equal probability. Language models are not the focus of this research and therefore are not discussed further.

2.3 Hidden Markov Models

HMMs are the acoustic models that produce the best results in speech recognition [5]. They estimate probabilities of sequences of events, and are comprised of states, where each state determines a set of probabilities. In general, HMMs are described by a state transition matrix, where each state has a transition probability of moving from the current state to the next state and also has probability densities of emitting continuous features from each state. An example of a three state HMM transition matrix is shown in Figure 2, where each number is a probability of going from the current state, represented by the rows, to the next state in the sequence, represented by the columns. For example, the value in row 2, column 3 represents the probability of moving from state 1 to state 2. The first row represents the initial or starting state, and the last row represents the final or exit state, which do not emit anything. The initial state is just a starting point, so the HMM cannot remain in the initial state and cannot return to the initial state once it is left, so the probabilities are zero for all of column 1. Similarly, once the exit state is reached, the HMM cannot transition to any other state, so the probabilities in row 5 are all zero.

In Figure 3 the arrows represent the probabilities governed by the state transition matrix. The i and e states are the initial and exit non-emitting states, and states 1, 2, and 3 are the emitting states. HMMs may use as many states as desired, although one to five is the norm for speech recognition. The more states that are used, the more complex an HMM model becomes, due to the fact that more parameters must be calculated to describe it. The parameters in the state transition matrix and the state emission probability densities begin with initial guesses, and training provides more accurate estimates of these parameters. The algorithm that accomplishes training by iteratively

$$
\begin{array}{c}
\text{next state} \\
\begin{array}{cccccc}
 & i & 1 & 2 & 3 & e
\end{array} \\
\begin{array}{c}
i \\
\text{current state } 1 \\
2 \\
3 \\
e
\end{array}
\begin{bmatrix}
0.0 & 1.0 & 0.0 & 0.0 & 0.0 \\
0.0 & 0.6 & 0.4 & 0.0 & 0.0 \\
0.0 & 0.0 & 0.6 & 0.4 & 0.0 \\
0.0 & 0.0 & 0.0 & 0.7 & 0.3 \\
0.0 & 0.0 & 0.0 & 0.0 & 0.0
\end{bmatrix}
\end{array}
$$

Figure 2. An example of a state transition matrix of an HMM.

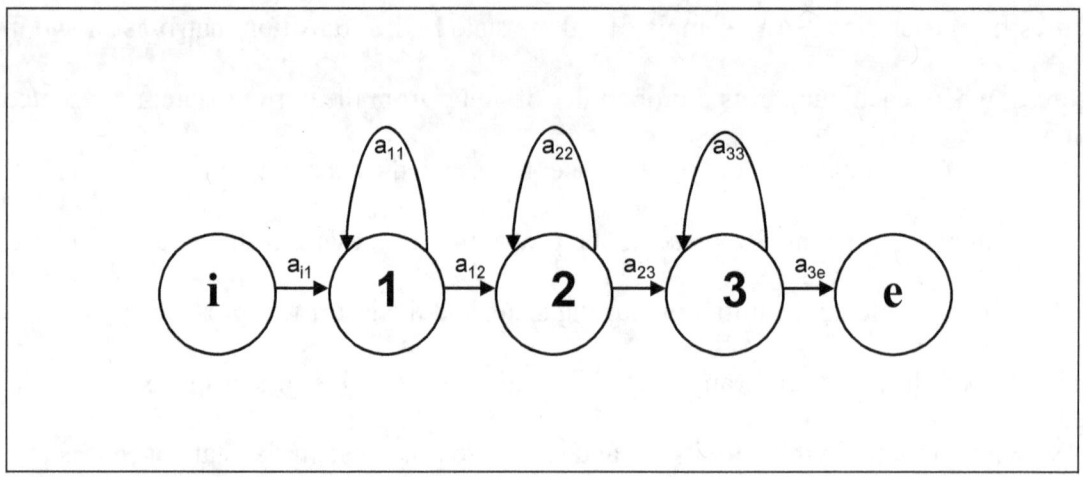

Figure 3. Diagram of a 3 state HMM with initial state and end state. The *a* variables represent state transition probabilities.

estimating and re-estimating these parameters is known as the Baum-Welch algorithm [4]. The Baum-Welch algorithm, also known as the Forward-Backward algorithm [5], is an expectation maximization algorithm that works iteratively to update the parameters of the HMMs to match the observed sequence of training data.

This research uses continuous density HMMs, which use a Gaussian probability density for each state to model the probability distribution of emitting continuous observation vectors from the HMM. The means and variances of these Gaussian mixture densities are estimated by the Baum-Welch algorithm for continuous HMMs using Equations 5-11. The probability of generating observation $\mathbf{v}_t$ in state j [4] is computed using Equation 5.

$$b_j\left(\mathbf{v}_t\right) = \sum_{m=1}^{M_j} c_{jm} N\left(\mathbf{v}_t; \mu_{jm}, \Sigma_{jm}\right), \tag{5}$$

where M_j is the number of mixture components in state j, c_{jm} is the weight of the m'th component and $N(\mathbf{v}_t; \mu, \Sigma)$ is a multivariate Gaussian density with mean vector μ and covariance matrix Σ, *i.e.*,

$$N\left(\mathbf{v};\mu,\Sigma\right) = \frac{1}{\sqrt{(2\pi)^n |\Sigma|}} e^{-\frac{1}{2}(\mathbf{v}-\mu)'\Sigma^{-1}(\mathbf{v}-\mu)}, \tag{6}$$

where n is the dimensionality of $\mathbf{v}$ [4] and $|\Sigma|$ denotes the determinant of the matrix Σ.

Next, the forward probability of observing the speech vectors while in state j at time t is estimated using Equation 7

$$\alpha_j(t) = \left[\sum_{i=2}^{N-1} \alpha_i(t-1)a_{ij}\right] b_j(\mathbf{v}_t), \tag{7}$$

where the state transition probability is a_{ij} [4]. The first and last states are the initial and exit states which do not emit; hence the limits of the summation do not include those states. Next, the backward probability [4] is estimated using Equation 8.

$$\beta_i(t) = \sum_{j=2}^{N-1} a_{ij} b_j(\mathbf{v}_{t+1})\beta_j(t+1), \tag{8}$$

where $\beta_i(t)$ is the probability that the model is in any state and will generate the remainder of the target sequence from time $= t + 1$ to time $= T$ [5]. The transition probabilities [4] are then able to be estimated using Equation 9.

$$a'_{ij} = \frac{\sum_{t=1}^{T} \alpha_i(t)a_{ij}b_j(\mathbf{v}_{t+1})\beta_j(t+1)}{\sum_{t=1}^{T} \alpha_i(t)\beta_i(t)} \tag{9}$$

Equations 10-11 describe the calculations for estimating the means and variances of the Gaussian mixtures. Each observation is weighted by $L_j(t)$, which is the probability of being in state j at time t, and normalized by dividing by the sum of all the L_j probabilities [4].

$$\mu'_j = \frac{\sum_{t=1}^{T} L_j(t)\mathbf{v}_t}{\sum_{t=1}^{T} L_j(t)} \tag{10}$$

$$\Sigma'_j = \frac{\sum_{t=1}^{T} L_j(t)(\mathbf{v}_t - \mu_j)(\mathbf{v}_t - \mu_j)'}{\sum_{t=1}^{T} Lj(t)} \qquad (11)$$

The set of equations described above can be used iteratively as many times as needed to get better estimates of the HMM parameters. In general, there is an equation for estimating the c_{jm} terms; however, this research used only single-mixture models for each state so the c_{jm} terms were all unity. For the speech recognition experiments performed here, the HMMs are trained with features extracted from the speech phonemes. Thousands of feature vectors are used as training data, and the result is one HMM that represents each individual phoneme.

Once the HMMs are trained, testing may begin. Testing classifies unknown phonemes by finding which HMM phoneme model is most likely to have produced the observed features. The test speech data are decoded using the HMMs along with a language model and a dictionary. Various algorithms exist for decoding the test speech data. The one employed in this project is known as the Viterbi algorithm [4]. The Viterbi algorithm is a dynamic programming algorithm that calculates the most likely set of HMM states that produced the observed set of sequences, which in this case is the test data, taking into account a language model and dictionary for computing results. For example, the algorithm takes a test speech input and computes the sequence of HMM phoneme models most likely to have produced it [5].

2.4 Mel Frequency Cepstral Coefficients as Features

Features often used for training HMMs are MFCCs [1] [4]. These are coefficients based on the Mel scale that represent sound. The word cepstral comes from the word cepstrum which is a logarithmic scale of the spectrum (and reverses the first four letters in the word spectrum). Figure 4 illustrates how MFCCs are calculated. First, the speech

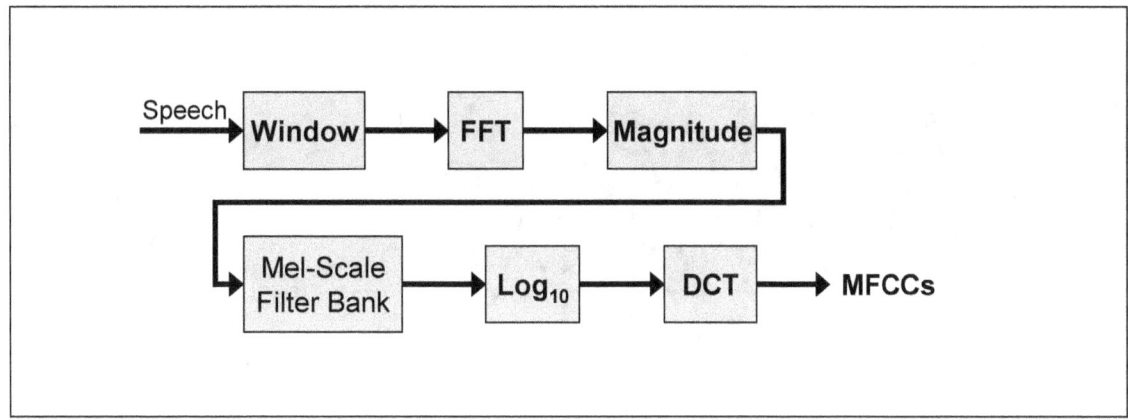

Figure 4. Block diagram of the calculations for MFCCs.

data are divided into 25 ms windows (frames). A new frame is started every 10 ms making this the sampling period and causing the windows to overlap each other. Next, the fast Fourier transform is performed on each frame of speech data and the magnitude is found. The next step involves filtering the signal with a frequency warped set of log filter banks called Mel-scale filter banks. These log filter banks collect the signal information into the coefficients m_i, which are the log filter bank amplitudes. The log filter banks are arranged along the frequency axis according to the Mel scale, a logarithmic scale that is a measure of perceived pitch or frequency of a tone [6], thus simulating the human hearing scale. The Mel scale is defined in Equation 12.

$$Mel(f) = 2595 \log_{10}\left(1 + \frac{f}{700}\right) \tag{12}$$

The Mel scale yields a compression of the upper frequencies where the human ear is less sensitive. The filtering process is illustrated in Figure 5. Next, the logarithm is taken of the log filter bank amplitudes. Finally, the MFCCs are calculated using the discrete cosine transform (DCT) in Equation 13.

11

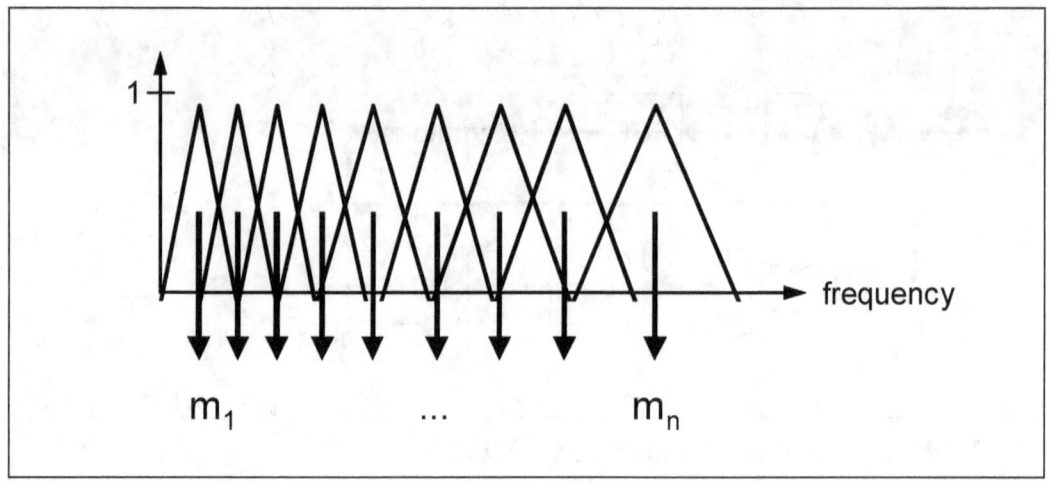

Figure 5. An example of a Mel-scale filter bank.

$$c_i = \sqrt{\frac{2}{N}} \sum_{j=1}^{N} m_j \cos\left(\frac{\pi i}{N}(j - 0.5)\right),$$ (13)

where N is the number of filter banks and the c_i terms are the resulting MFCCs.

To further enhance speech recognition performance, an extra set of delta and acceleration coefficient features are sometimes calculated with MFCCs. These features are the first and second time derivatives of the original coefficients, respectively.

The results obtained in this project are compared to speech recognition performance on regular MFCCs as well as on MFCCs with delta and acceleration coefficients. Generally, the MFCC method for ASR yields the most successful results.

2.5 Auditory Image Model

An alternative method of feature extraction that is a more recent development than MFCCs is something called the Auditory Image Model (AIM). The AIM model is software that models how the human ear processes speech [7]. It models the human hearing mechanism by simulating the processes the ear performs on a sound, resulting in an auditory image that represents the sound. AIM includes tools to simulate the spectral analysis, neural encoding, and temporal integration performed by the auditory system [7].

Figure 6 shows a block diagram that represents the process that AIM uses to process a sound. The PCP (pre-cochlear processing) block performs filtering of the signal to represent the response up to the oval window of the inner ear. The BMM (basilar membrane motion) block represents the basilar membrane motion response to the signal. It is simulated by a gamma-tone filter bank of bandpass filters with evenly distributed center frequencies along a quasi-logarithmic scale known as an equivalent rectangular bandwidth (ERB) scale [8]. This process transforms the signal (in effect) to a moving surface that represents the basilar membrane as a function of time [9]. The NAP (neural activity pattern) block simulates the neural activity pattern produced by basilar membrane energy transduction to the auditory nerve which generates its firing activity pattern [7].

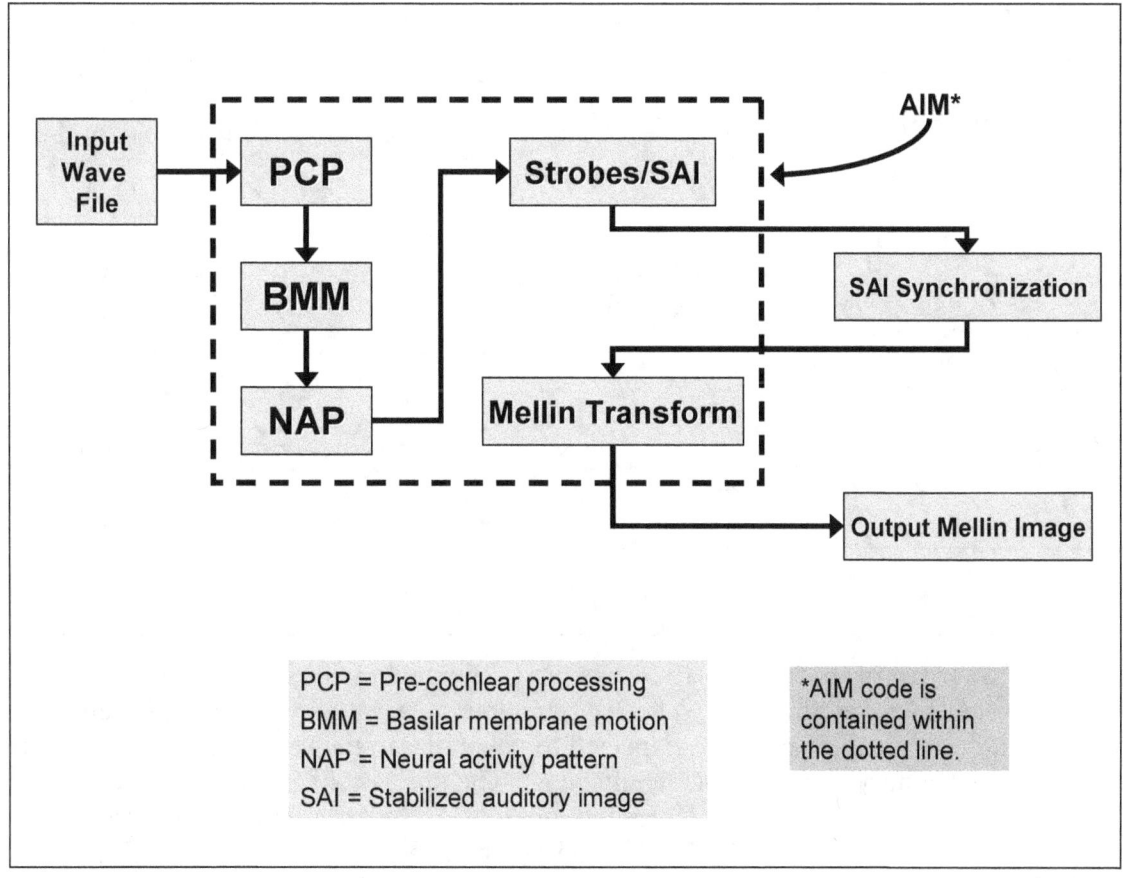

Figure 6. A block diagram of AIM and each of its modules.

Figure 7 shows one frame of the NAP of a speech signal. The pulses have a rightward skew from high to low frequency (as shown by the dotted lines) because of the phase lag in the output of the cochlea in the BMM [7].

The Strobes/SAI (stabilized auditory image) block calculates the stabilized auditory image using strobed temporal integration (STI) and represents the temporal integration performed on the NAP. This process simulates the perception of the human ear by stabilizing oscillating sounds into static patterns [7]. STI works by strobing the

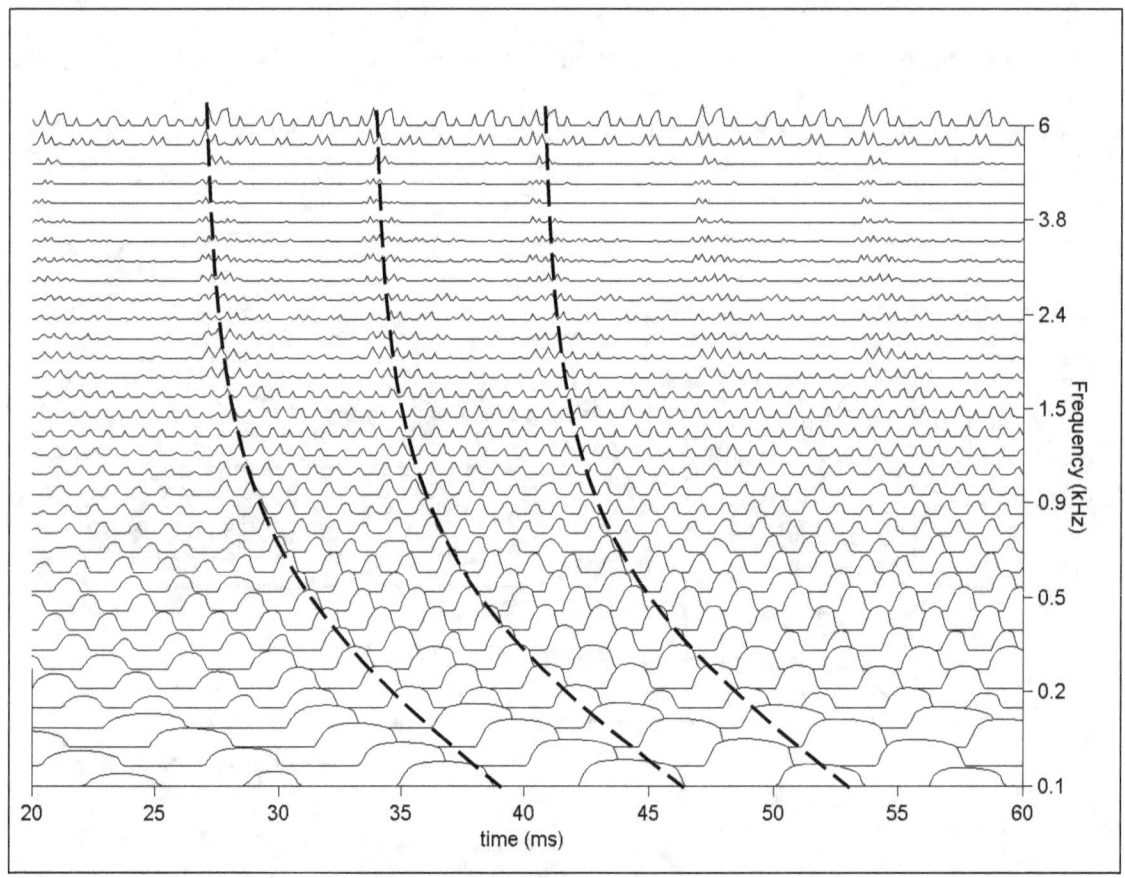

Figure 7. A frame of the NAP of a vowel sound generated by the NAP block of Figure 6 and presented as a waterfall plot. The NAP module of AIM converts basilar membrane motion into a representation that is expected to be similar to the pattern of neural activity found in the auditory nerve or cochlea nucleus. The abscissa of the plot is time, and on the ordinate each horizontal line represents one of 35 channels with center frequencies from 100 Hz to 6 kHz on a log scale. The height of each pulse represents the "firing rate" of the NAP.

14

signal to the levels of high activity in the NAP by locating the points in each channel that are local maxima. This information then defines the limits of integration when performing temporal integration for calculating the SAI [8]. Figure 8 shows one frame of the SAI of the speech signal from Figure 7. The SAI representation is based on the assumption that as the NAP flows from the cochlea, the human hearing mechanism acts as a bank of delay line filters [10] that capture information into a buffer store. This process stabilizes the repeating patterns of the NAP into the SAI, which is an image representing the sound. The phase lag from the NAP plot is removed, causing the phase

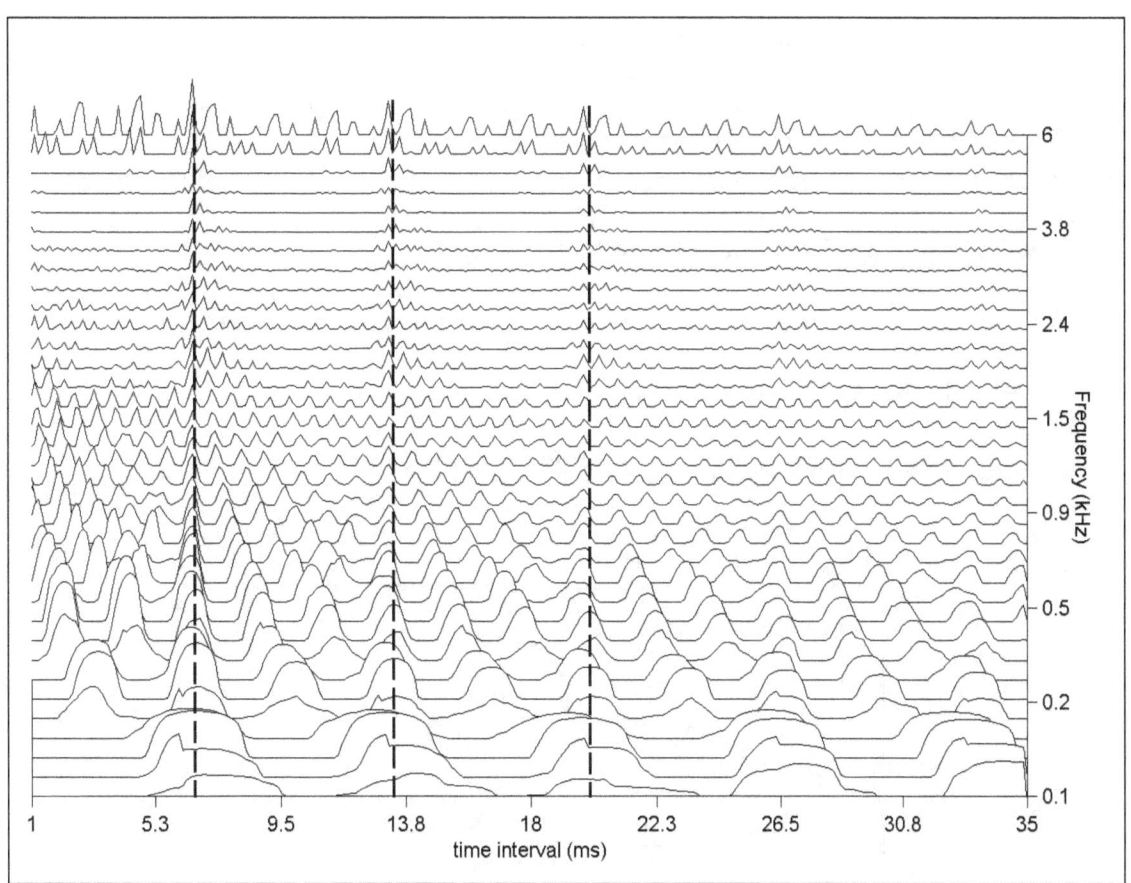

Figure 8. A frame of the stabilized auditory image (SAI) of a vowel sound generated by the AIM. The SAI module of AIM uses STI to convert the NAP into the SAI. The abscissa of the plot is time, the ordinate is frequency on a log scale, and vertical height represents the "firing rate" of the SAI.

to be aligned in the SAI plot as shown by the dotted lines. The SAI is described by Equation 14 as

$$A_I\left(\alpha f_0, \tau\right) = \sum_{k=0}^{\infty} S_w\left(\alpha f_0, \tau + kt_p\right) e^{-\xi\tau} e^{-\eta kt_p}, \qquad (14)$$

where S_w is the output of the NAP, αf_0 is the peak frequency of each auditory filter in the filter bank, τ is the time axis for the SAI, t_p is the period of the signal, and η and ξ are factors that affect the time interval of each SAI frame and the decay rate of the waveforms in each frame [11]. The pattern of the pulse peaks or ridges in the SAI follow a time-interval-peak frequency product path, denoted by h, which is constant along the ridges of the SAI. This time interval-peak frequency product path is used later in the calculation of the MT. The SAI synchronization block and its justification are discussed in Section 3.2.2.

2.6 The Mellin Transform and its Applications

The MT is the integral transform defined in Equation 1. Similar to the Fourier transform (FT), the MT possesses certain properties [12], some of which are displayed in Table 2. As mentioned previously, the scaling property of the MT is exploited in this

Property	Function	Mellin Transform
Standard	$f(t)$	$M(s)$
Scaling	$f(at)$	$a^{-s}M(s)$
Linear	$af(t)$	$a\,M(s)$
Translation	$x^a f(t)$	$M(a+s)$
Exponentiation	$f(t^a)$	$a^{-1}\,M(s/a)$

Table 2. Key properties of the MT. The property of interest here is the scaling property, which states that dilation of the abscissa in the time-domain by the factor a has no effect on the shape of $M(s)$ in the Mellin-domain. The time dilation by a is encoded in the a^{-s} factor and does not dilate $M(s)$.

project. The FT is translation-invariant in that it does not matter if the signal is shifted in time by some Δt; the magnitude of the FT of the signal remains the same (although the phase changes). This translation invariance does not hold for the MT, however, so the limits of integration must be defined when it is calculated. The limits of integration are defined by the STI, as discussed in the previous section. The MT is not translation invariant, but it has a scaling property, and when evaluated under certain conditions it is scale invariant within a phase factor [11] [3]. This scale invariance comes from the scaling property of the MT and means that as the time-domain distribution of the signal is subjected to dilation, the magnitude distribution of the MT does not dilate. Contrast this to the FT, where if the time axis of a signal is compressed or expanded, the magnitude of the Fourier spectrum is expanded or compressed, respectively. However, for the MT, dilation of the time-axis does not compress or expand the distribution in the Mellin domain. Equations 15-17 show how the scaling property of the MT, affects time axis dilation of a signal. In particular, let

$$M_{f(t)}(s) = \int_0^\infty t^{s-1} f(t)\, dt.$$ (15)

If the time axis is dilated by a factor of a, the result is

$$M_{f(at)}(s) = \int_0^\infty t^{s-1} f(at)\, dt.$$ (16)

With $\tau = at$, or $t = \tau/a$, the integral is:

$$\int_0^\infty \left(\frac{\tau}{a}\right)^{s-1} f(\tau)\frac{d\tau}{a} \; = \; \left(\frac{1}{a}\right)^{s-1}\left(\frac{1}{a}\right)\int_0^\infty \tau^{s-1} f(\tau)\, d\tau \; = \; a^{-s} M_{f(t)}(s).$$ (17)

Thus, if $M(s)$ is the MT of some function $f(t)$, the introduction of a dilation factor a either expands or compresses the time axis, but in the Mellin domain the net result of the MT is a segregation of the size and shape information from the signal [11]. This normalizing effect of the MT may be useful for achieving improved speaker independent speech recognition. Figure 9 shows the MT of the SAI from Figure 8. Chapter 3 gives an in-depth description of how the MT is calculated in Matlab, which indicated that the MT is evaluated using an FT such that $s = -jc + \frac{1}{2}$.

The MT has many uses, including digital image registration and digital watermarking [13], digital audio effects processing [14], and vowel normalization [11]. Experiments in vowel normalization have shown positive results [3]. Thus, this research attempts to use the normalizing effect of the MT on all speech to determine if results improve over conventional ASR methods.

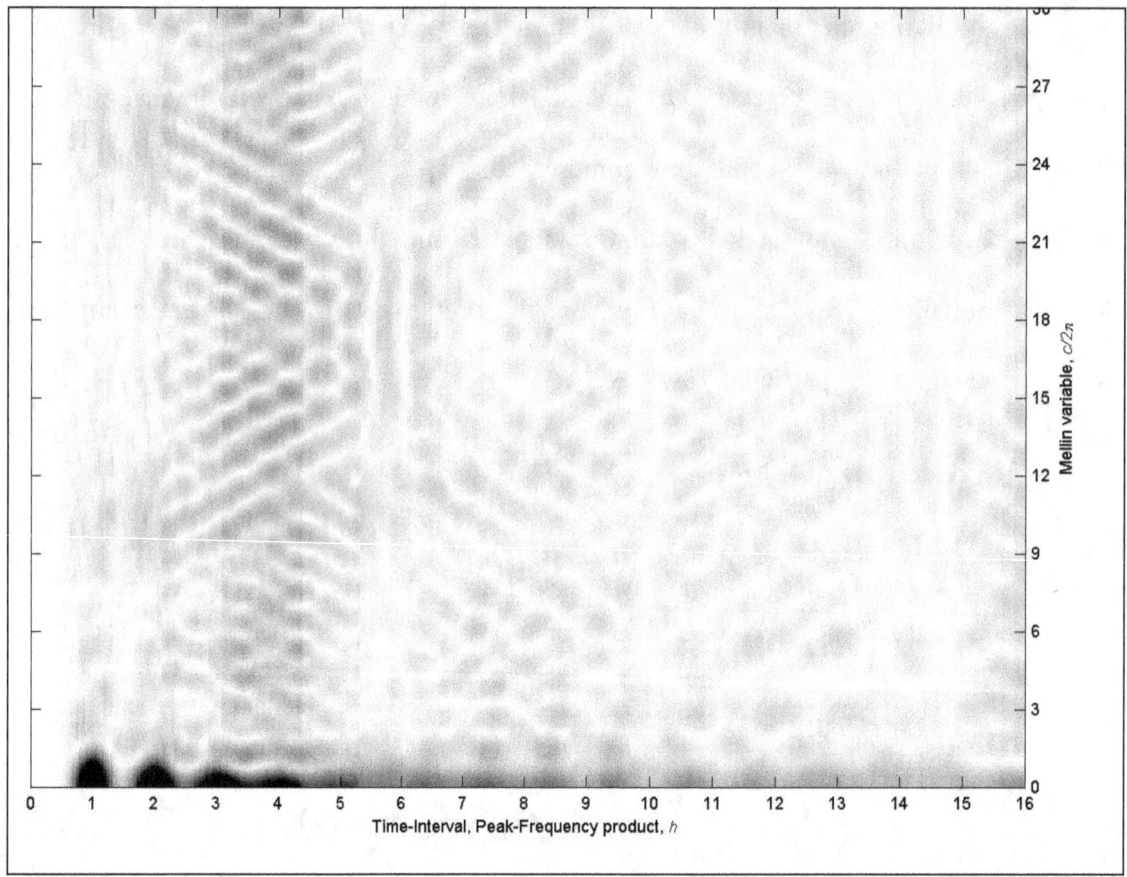

Figure 9. A section of the MT of the SAI from Figure 8 generated by the MT block of the AIM. The abscissa of the plot is called the time-interval-peak frequency product because the ridges in the SAI plot follow a path where the time-interval and the peak frequency in the SAI equal a constant, h. The MT is computed along these vertical paths, which results in a two-dimensional MT plot. The ordinate shows the Mellin variable, which is the argument of the MT, much like $j\omega$ in the FT. Darker color in a region indicates greater Mellin coefficient magnitude.

III.   Experimental Design

This section presents the steps taken for phoneme recognition experiments with MFCCs and the MT features using HMMs trained with the Hidden Markov Model toolkit (HTK) [15]. The experiments were run using the TIMIT database.

3.1 TIMIT Database

The TIMIT database is a collection of 6300 sentences, 10 sentences each spoken by 630 persons from eight different dialect regions in the United States. The speech was recorded at Texas Instruments (TI) and transcribed at the Massachusetts Institute of Technology (MIT), which is how the database derives its name. It was created for the purpose of "providing speech data for the acquisition of acoustic-phonetic knowledge and for the development and evaluation of automatic speech recognition systems" [16]. The database is divided into training data, which consists of approximately 73% of the database, and testing data, which consists of approximately 27% of the database. The transcription files containing the words and phonemes of each spoken sentence are also contained in the database.

For some experiments, a subset of the database is used instead of the entire database. This subset consists of 100 sentences, 10 spoken utterances each from 10 speakers. For the subset, training is performed by the leave one out method which trains on 9 speakers and tests on the 10th speaker, then leaves a different speaker out for testing, etc. The results of leaving each speaker out once is averaged and shown as the result. The reason for using this subset was to obtain some results quickly from each of the experiments before performing them on the entire database, which requires much more time.

TIMIT is a small sized database by current standards, but it is a good choice for this research because it is a diverse collection of data that possesses a good balance between having enough data for training and testing and being small enough to avoid an exorbitant amount of time in running experiments. It also is useful for speech recognition research because it has been in existence for over two decades, has been used in numerous experiments, and can be used for comparison with results obtained here.

3.2 Mellin Transform Processing

Several versions of the AIM exist. For this research, the Auditory Image Model in Matlab (*aim-mat*) [7] is used to implement the AIM, because it is the only version that includes code for performing the MT. *Aim-mat* has a graphical user interface (GUI) which allows a user to load a sound file and perform AIM calculations on it with ease; however, this research employs the command line version of *aim-mat* instead of the GUI to receive input and produce results so that batch processing can be implemented without user interaction. A parameter structure file called "all_parameters.m" (listed in Appendix A) includes all necessary parameters for the AIM calculations. When run in Matlab, this structure file creates a variable called "all_options", which specifies various parameters and options necessary for each block of AIM.

3.2.1 Processing up to the SAI Stage

Figure 10 shows the overall process. The first step is to convert the speech files in the TIMIT database, which are NIST sphere files, to wave file format so that Matlab can use them. This conversion is accomplished using the Perl script "convert_timit_wav.pl" (listed in Appendix B). The Matlab script "main_program.m" (listed in Appendix C) was developed to use the *aim-mat* code by calling the appropriate functions, processing the resulting data from these functions, and writing results to the

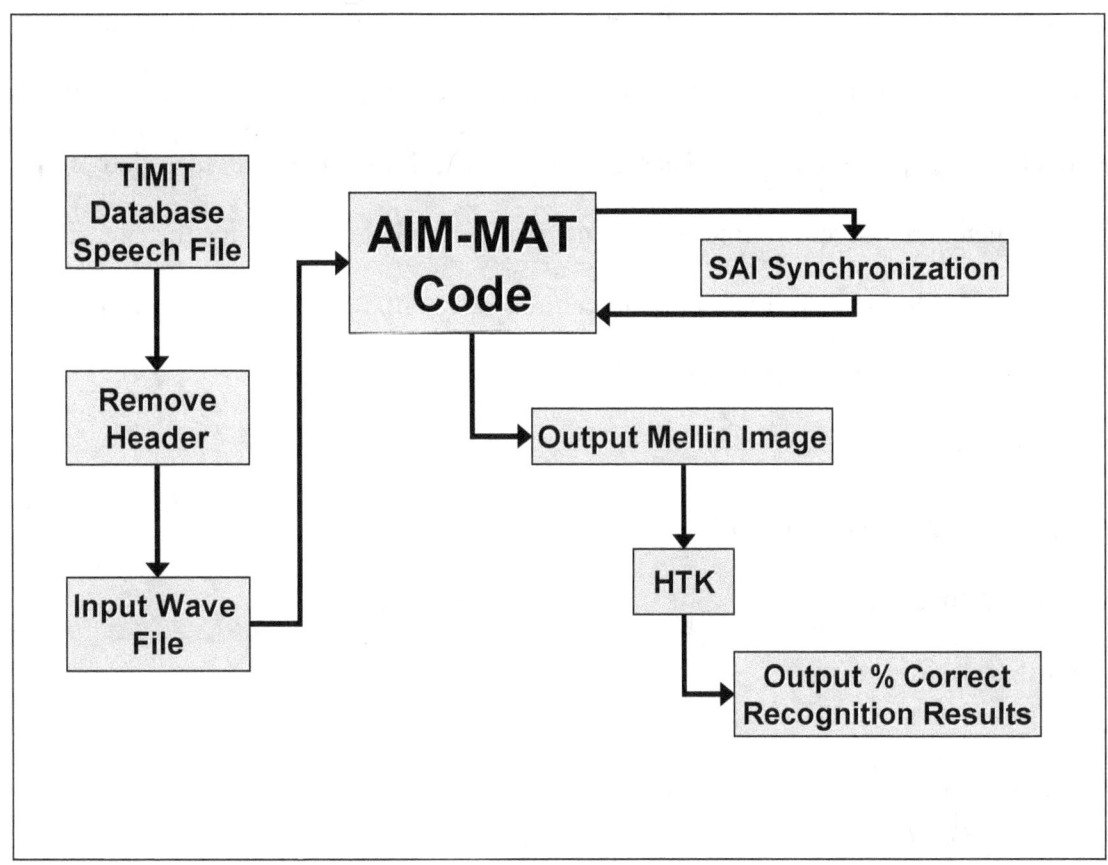

Figure 10. Block diagram of the overall procedure. Data from the TIMIT database is first preprocessed so that it is useable in Matlab. The aim-mat code uses the resulting input wave files to construct the SAI and the MT of the SAI. A modification made to the code written specifically for this research is represented by the SAI synchronization block. This module converts the SAI, which is asynchronous, into a synchronous data stream before the MT is computed and the MT images are sent to HTK for recognition tests. The HMMs require synchronous data for training.

correct location. Thus, the "main_program.m" script runs the entire process of the conversion from wave files to Mellin transform data files, including loading the parameter file, calling the *aim-mat* subroutines, loading SAI and MT image data, saving SAI and MT image data, plotting, and converting MT image data to HTK format. The paths in the "main_program.m" script must be set correctly to read from the directory where the wave files are stored and to write the SAI and MT results in the desired directory. The options in the "main_program.m" script can be set so that only the SAI is calculated, only the MT is calculated (on previously calculated SAI), both SAI and MT are calculated on the fly, or the HTK conversion of the previously calculated MT files is calculated. The parameters for each of the six AIM modules are specified in the "all_parameters.m" script. Some of the parameters include specifying the algorithms used in the AIM modules. Each module can use different algorithms to accomplish the calculation. The built-in algorithms used here are:

- PCP: none

- BMM: gamma-tone filter bank

- NAP: irinonap

- Strobes: irinostrobes

- SAI: irinosai

- User-Module: mellin

These algorithms perform the steps in the AIM (as discussed in Section 2.5), as well as the MT. They were chosen because they are less computationally intensive than alternative algorithms. Future research could investigate the effects of different choices for the various components.

Once all the parameters and options are set, the "main_program.m" script uses the *aim-mat* code to generate the AIM of the speech signals, which includes its SAI and the MT of the SAI. The SAI is a representation of the speech signal that is divided into frames, where each frame represents 35 ms of the speech signal.

3.2.2 SAI Synchronization

The SAI representation is asynchronous, meaning that the time intervals between the start-times of each frame are not the same. Later, HMMs are used to perform the speech recognition experiments, and they require synchronous input data. Therefore, the

SAI must be synchronized prior to the experiments. The SAI synchronization block from Figure 6 represents this step, which is performed before the MT calculation. The script called "synch_sai.m" (listed in Appendix D) is additional code, written specifically for this research, to execute the SAI synchronization process. It works by sampling the SAI every 10ms and taking the frame that starts the closest to each 10 ms sampling period. The sampling rate of 10 ms was chosen because it equals the sampling rate used for calculating MFCCs. By using the same sampling rate for both MFCC calculation and SAI synchronization calculation, results can be more accurately compared between both methods. This SAI synchronization process discards some of the original frames, which is acceptable because portions of each of the frames representing the speech signal overlap. Each frame contains an image with six to eight vertical pulse patterns called strobes, where each strobe contains a decayed version of the previous strobe. The synchronization processes each frame by taking only the first 10 ms, which is approximately the first two strobes of each SAI frame, because each frame contains a decayed part of the frame previous to it. By removing the decayed portions from each frame, the synchronized SAI contains less redundant information than the original SAI. This action also has the benefit of a reduction in computation time for the MT calculation. Figure 11 shows a synchronized version of the SAI.

3.2.3 Mellin Transform Calculation

After the necessary synchronization process is complete, the final step in the *aim-mat* code performs the calculations for the MT, and the results are saved to the previously specified path in the "main_program.m" script.

Aim-mat uses the MT to map auditory speech images from vocal tracts of different sizes into an invariant MT image [17] by performing a one dimensional MT

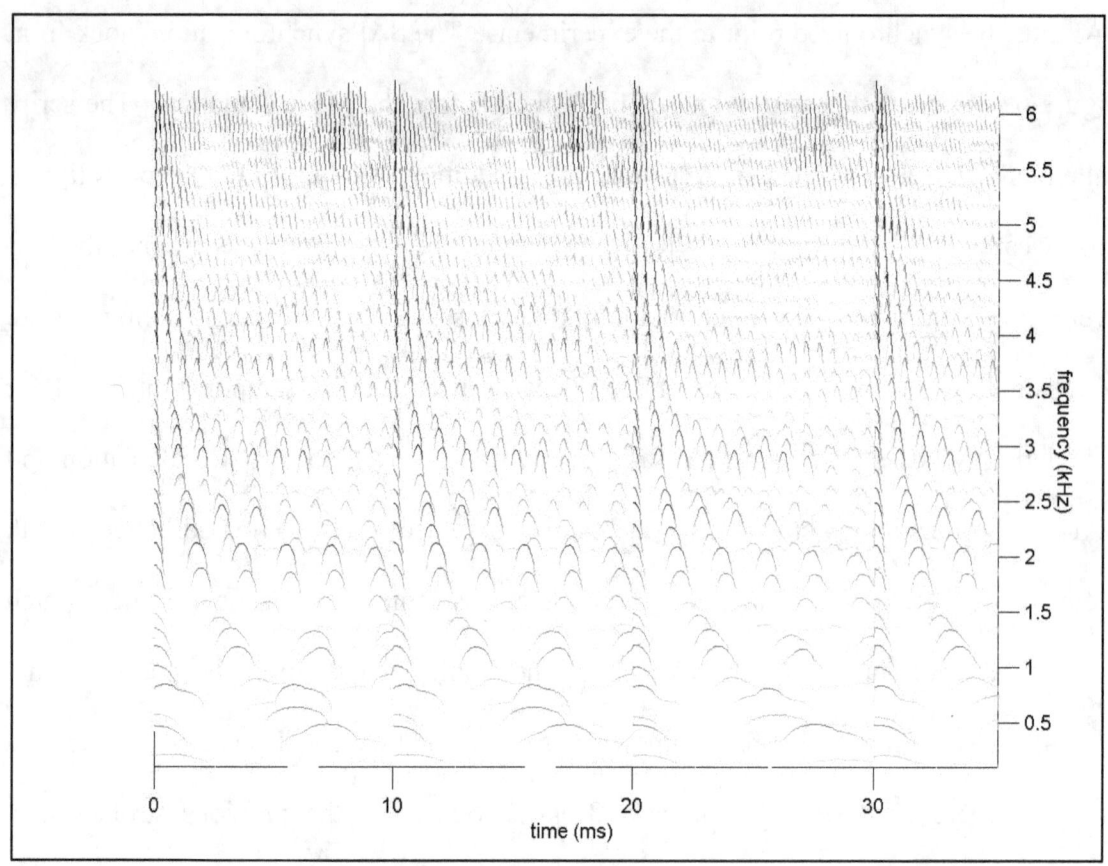

Figure 11. The sampled version of the SAI generated by the "SAI synchronization" code. Each strobe begins at each multiple of 10 ms, which is due to the 10 ms sampling rate of the synchronization process. The process also takes the first two strobes from each frame and removes the rest, which is a decayed version of the first 2 strobes. The abscissa of the plot is time, the ordinate is frequency on a log scale, and vertical height represents the "firing rate" of the SAI.

along each time interval-peak frequency product column of the SAI, resulting in a collection of MTs which form a two-dimensional image. The MT of the SAI [11] from Equation 14 is

$$M(s,h) = \int_0^T A_I\left(\frac{h}{\tau}, \tau\right) e^{(s-1)\ln\tau} d\tau, \tag{18}$$

where A_I is the SAI representation and h is the parameter representing the time interval-peak frequency product constant.

24

Calculation of the MT image from the SAI is accomplished by a two stage process. First, a time dilation of each of the SAI channels by a factor proportional to the center frequency of the channel filter is performed. This intermediate representation is called the size-shape image (SSI) [17] and implements the $\ln \tau$ term in Equation 18 by creating a log-time axis [11]. The logarithmic time scale is achieved if we let

$$t = e^x, \quad dt = e^x dx, \quad 0 \rightarrow -\infty, \quad \infty \rightarrow \infty .$$

This causes the form of the MT when evaluated at $s = -jc + \frac{1}{2}$ to be

$$
\left.
\begin{aligned}
M_{f(t)}\left(-jc+1/2\right) &= \int_0^\infty e^{-jc-x-1/2} f\left(e^x\right) e^x \, dx \\[2mm]
&= \int_0^\infty e^{-jcx} e^{-1/2} f\left(e^x\right) dx \\[2mm]
&= \frac{1}{e^{1/2}} \int_0^\infty e^{-jcx} f\left(e^x\right) dx
\end{aligned}
\right\},
\tag{19}
$$

which is the FT on a logarithmic time scale. This is used in the second state where the SSI is used to compute the MT. The center frequencies of the AIM filters are now on a logarithmic scale along the abscissa. This coordinate system makes the MT equivalent to a FT on spatial frequency [11], where each column of the final MT image is computed by performing the FT on the columns of the SSI [17] and taking the magnitude.

3.3 Illustration of the Effect of Pitch Scaling

Generally women and children have higher pitched voices than men. Figures 12 and 13 use this fact to illustrate the effects of pitch scaling on the MT by showing a simulated vowel sound at pitches of 100 Hz and 200 Hz, respectively. This pitch difference simulates how typical male and female voices produce the same vowel sound with different pitches. The first, second, and third formants, indicated by the horizontal arrows in both figures, are at a frequency of 450 Hz, 1450 Hz, and 2450 Hz, respectively, simulating the formants of the phoneme /uh/. It can be seen that the pitch periods for the male spoken vowel of Figure 12 last approximately twice the amount of time as those for the female spoken vowel of Figure 13, as indicated by the vertical arrows in each figure.

Figures 14 and 15 show the MT of Figures 12 and 13, respectively. It can be seen that the high amplitude regions for Figure 14 lie in the same regions as those of Figure 15. The differences in the amplitudes are due to the fact that the two vowels are not fully scaled versions of each other. Only the pitch is scaled; the formants are the same for the two signals.

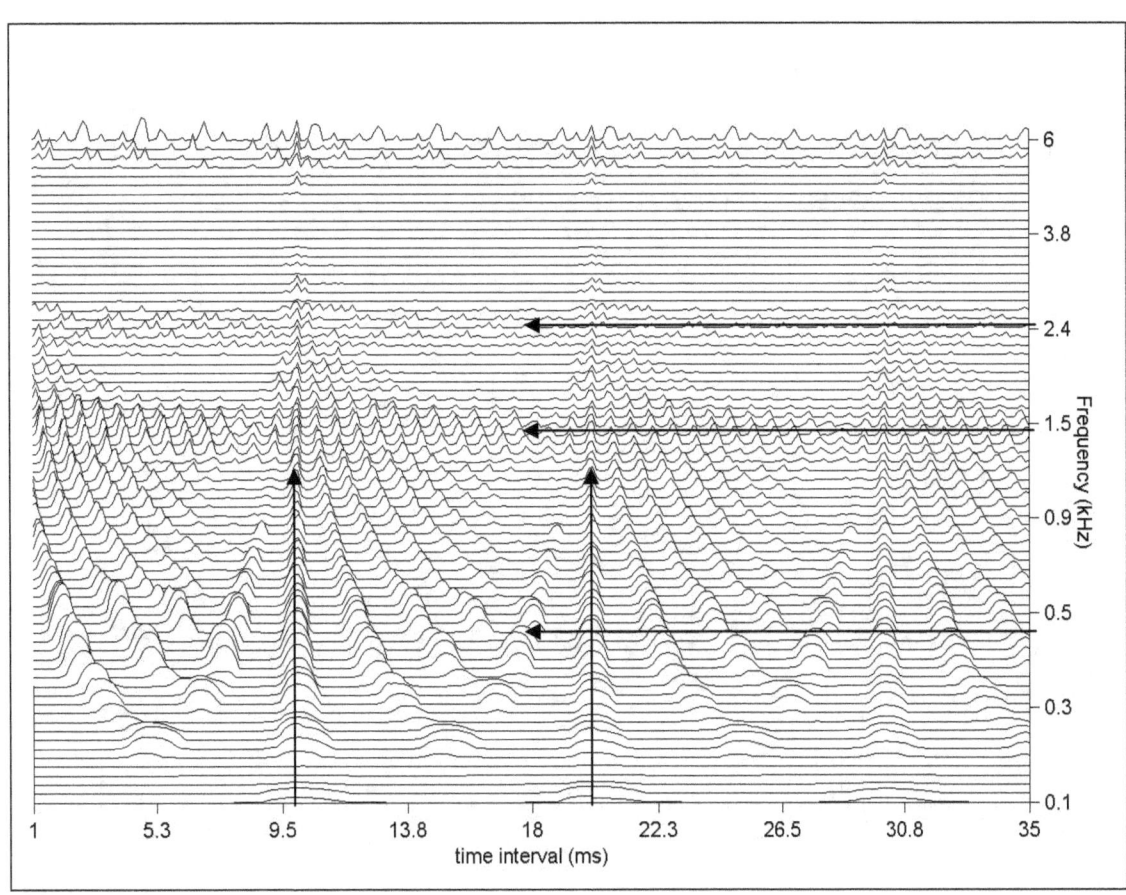

Figure 12. The SAI of the vowel sound /uh/ at a pitch of 100 Hz, typical of a male speaker. Notice that the pitch period is 10 ms as indicated by the vertical arrows. The vowel formants are 450 Hz, 1450 Hz, and 2450 Hz as shown by the horizontal arrows. Compare this figure to Figure 13, which shows the same vowel spoken with a pitch of 200 Hz, typical of a female speaker.

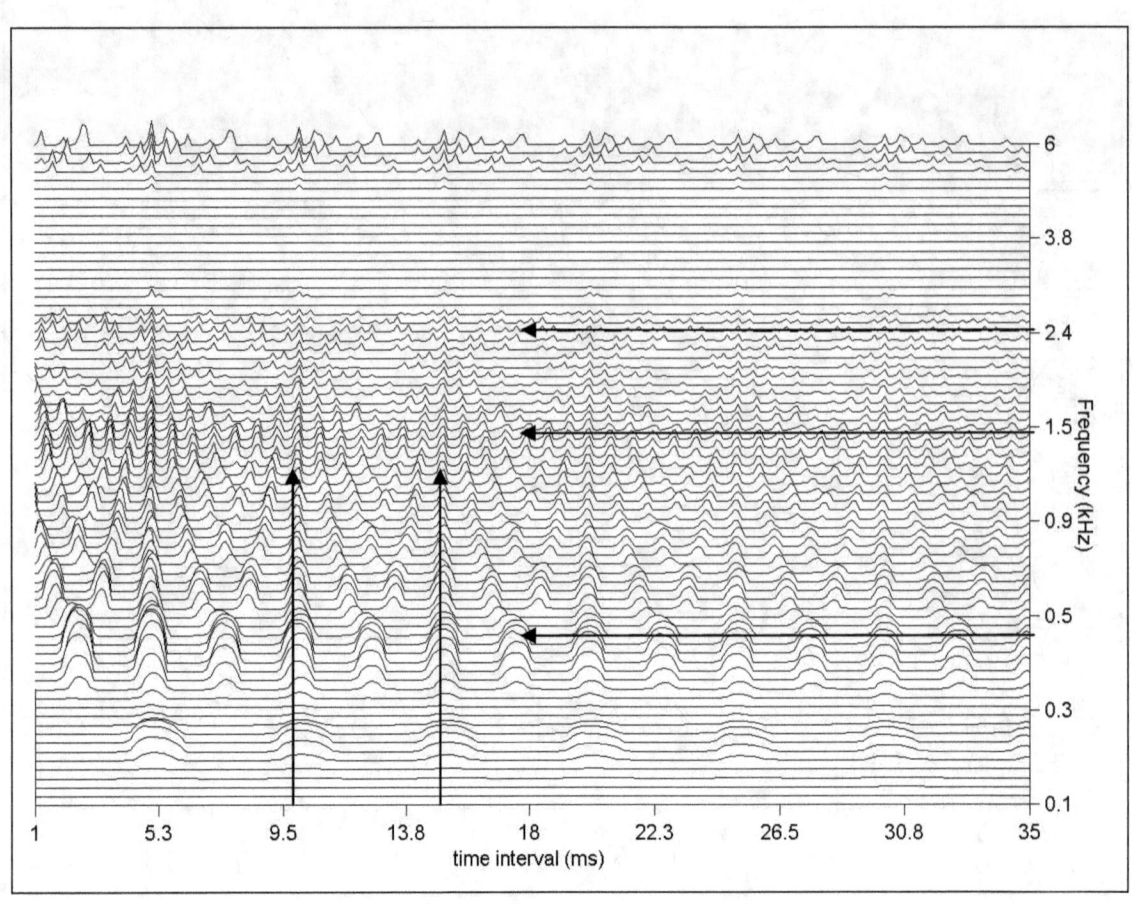

Figure 13. The SAI of the vowel sound /uh/ at a pitch of 200 Hz, typical of a female speaker. Notice the pitch period is 5 ms as indicated by the vertical arrows.

28

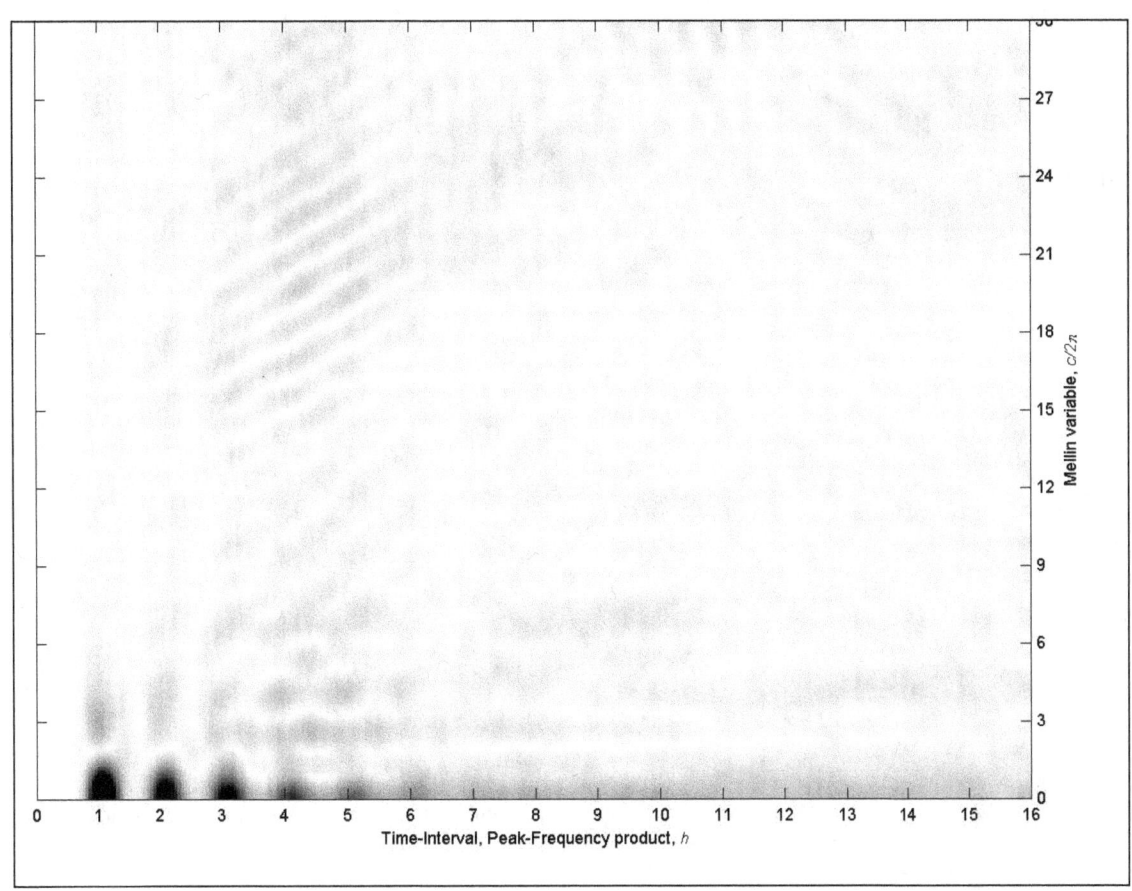

Figure 14. The MT of the SAI from Figure 12. Compare this plot to Figure 15, which is
the MT of the SAI from Figure 13.

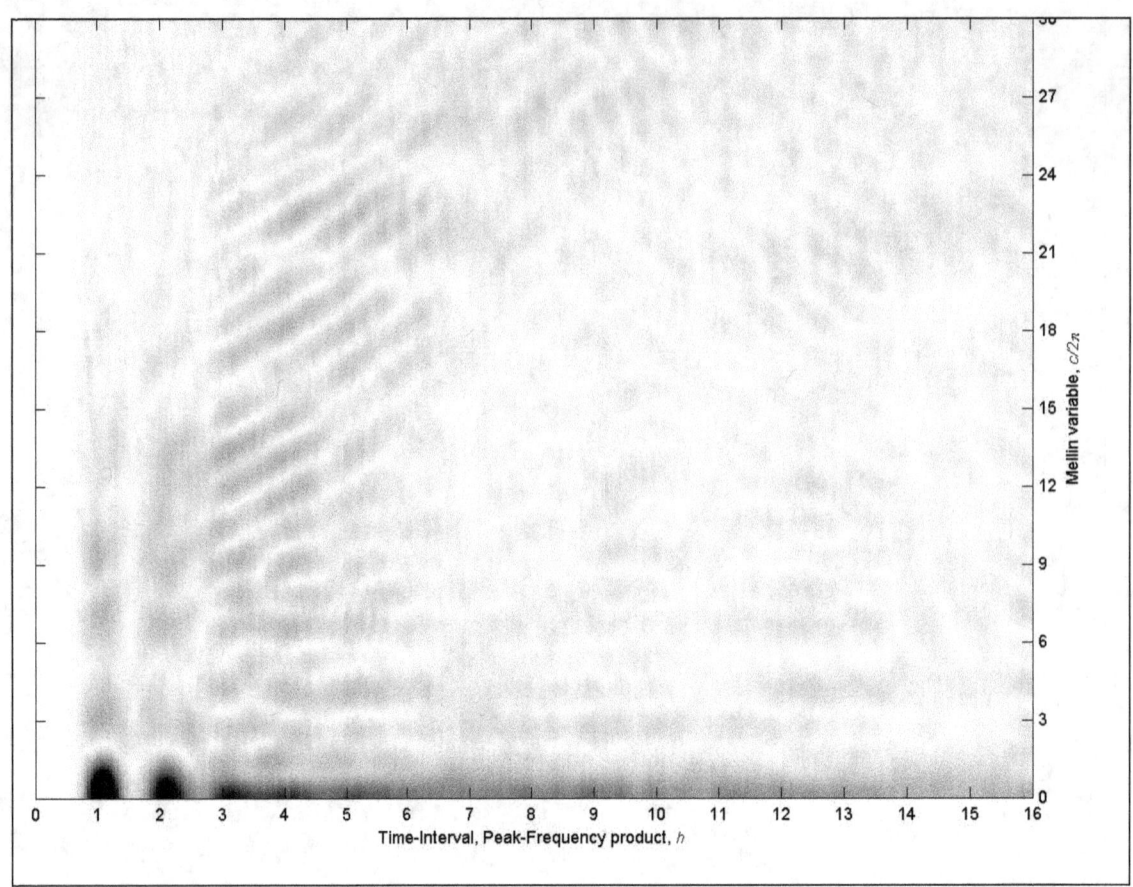

Figure 15. The MT of the SAI from Figure 13. Figures 12 and 13 show considerable changes between male and female vowels, whereas Figures 14 and 15 show similar regions of high amplitude.

30

3.4 HMMs with HTK

This research uses a set of programs called HTK to train HMMs and conduct phoneme recognition experiments. HTK is open source software designed by the Cambridge University Engineering Department along with Entropic Research Laboratories [15]. HTK also provides utilities for extracting features from speech data and custom user defined features can be imported into HTK, as was the case for this project.

Before the MT data can be used in HTK to perform speech recognition experiments, it must be converted to a format that HTK can use. The Matlab script "writehtk.m", obtained from the Imperial College department of electrical and electronic engineering at the University of London website [18], is used to perform the conversion of MT data to HTK format. This conversion is accomplished by reshaping the matrices of each MT frame into a row vector so that each frame is one row. The data is written as a floating point binary file. The frame period, which is 10 ms, is also encoded into the file along with a flag identifying the data as user defined features. After this process, the data can be imported into HTK.

Figure 16 illustrates the processes and commands used to perform phoneme recognition. The HCopy command is part of the data preparation phase and calculates MFCC features of the input speech data. Because data preparation for the MT is accomplished prior to importing into HTK, the HCopy command is not needed for the MT features and is omitted. The next command in HTK is HCompV, which works by computing the global mean and covariance of the training data and assigning these values as the starting points in the Gaussians in each phoneme HMM model. This assignment is known as the initialization stage for "flat-start" training, because each phoneme model

31

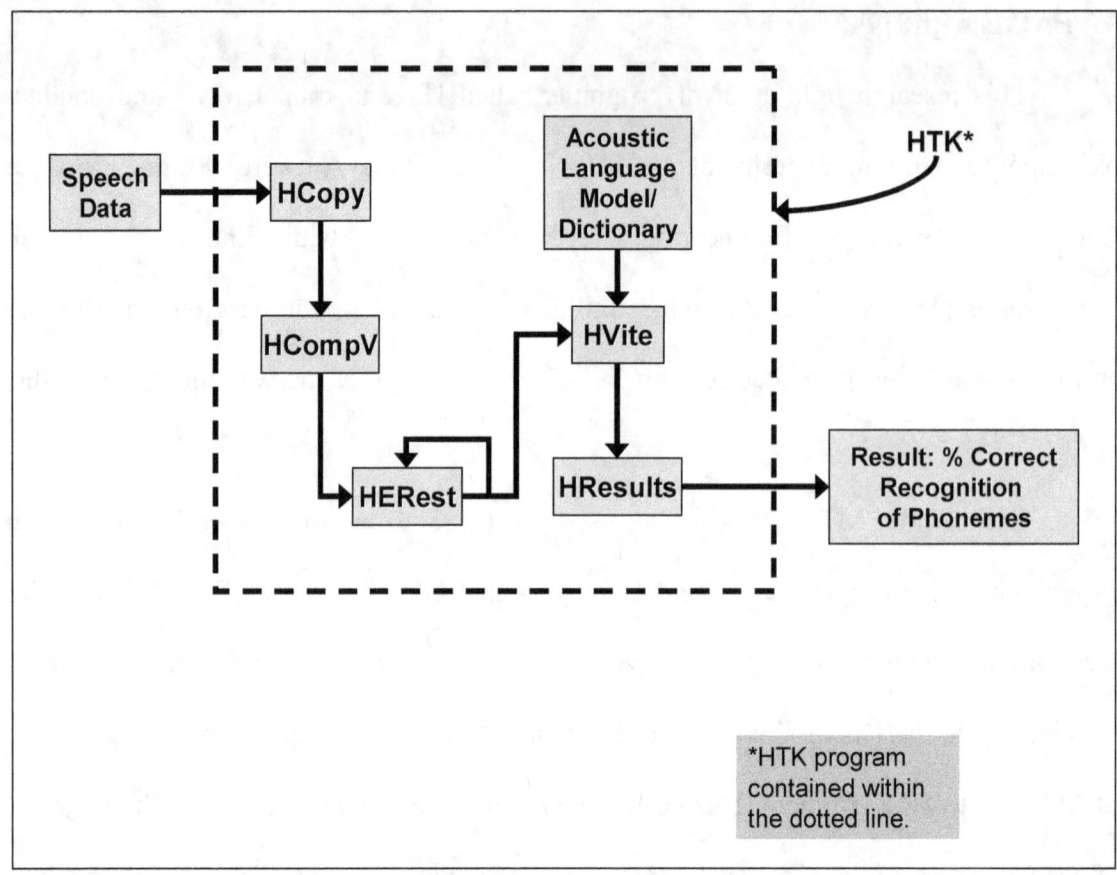

Figure 16. A block diagram for steps HTK uses in taking an input and computing percent correct recognition results. Results can be shown in percent correct recognition per sentence, per speaker, or over the entire test data set.

starts identically [4]. Once initial estimates for the HMM models are calculated, the models can be re-estimated by training with the HERest command. This command uses the Baum-Welch algorithm to perform re-estimation of the mean, variance and state transition parameters of the HMMs [4] and may be used iteratively to re-estimate the parameters of the HMM models. For this research, the re-estimation is performed for a total of three iterations. In iteratively estimating the HMM parameters, there is the option of updating the weights, means, and variances of the mixtures. For some of the experiments, a global variance was used and not further updated.

When training is complete, the HVite command is used for testing. HVite is a Viterbi word recognizer that computes the likelihood of the phonemes that produced the given speech data using the HMM models, a language model, and a dictionary, and it outputs a transcription of the speech file. When testing is complete, the HResults command outputs the results, including the percent correct recognition rates as well as other statistics determined by options in the command. Some of these statistics include: the number of correctly recognized phonemes, words, and sentences as well as the number of errors from deletions, insertions, and substitutions. Also, HResults can compute a confusion matrix, which is a matrix that displays all phonemes in rows that show which phoneme is recognized and the number of times it occurs.

Several variations of test data are used for the training and test process in this project. By default the MT produced by the AIM has too many features to estimate with HTK (about 192,000); however the options in the "main_program.m" file can be set to control the MT image data resolution. The number of features and the size of the MT image file are equivalent to image resolution, where a larger resolution means that more pixels are required to describe the image, resulting in a larger memory requirement. Smaller images reduce the memory size of the image but also reduce the information contained in the image, as illustrated in Figure 17, which show the two Mellin image resolutions used here compared to the default resolution that aim-mat produces. HTK was recompiled to accept a maximum number of features of 8192. Due to this limitation, the original number of features set in the options file for the MT data was 8100. The use of 500 features from the MT was also investigated, to make the process of training and testing faster and to observe the impact of the reduced resolution on the recognition results. The

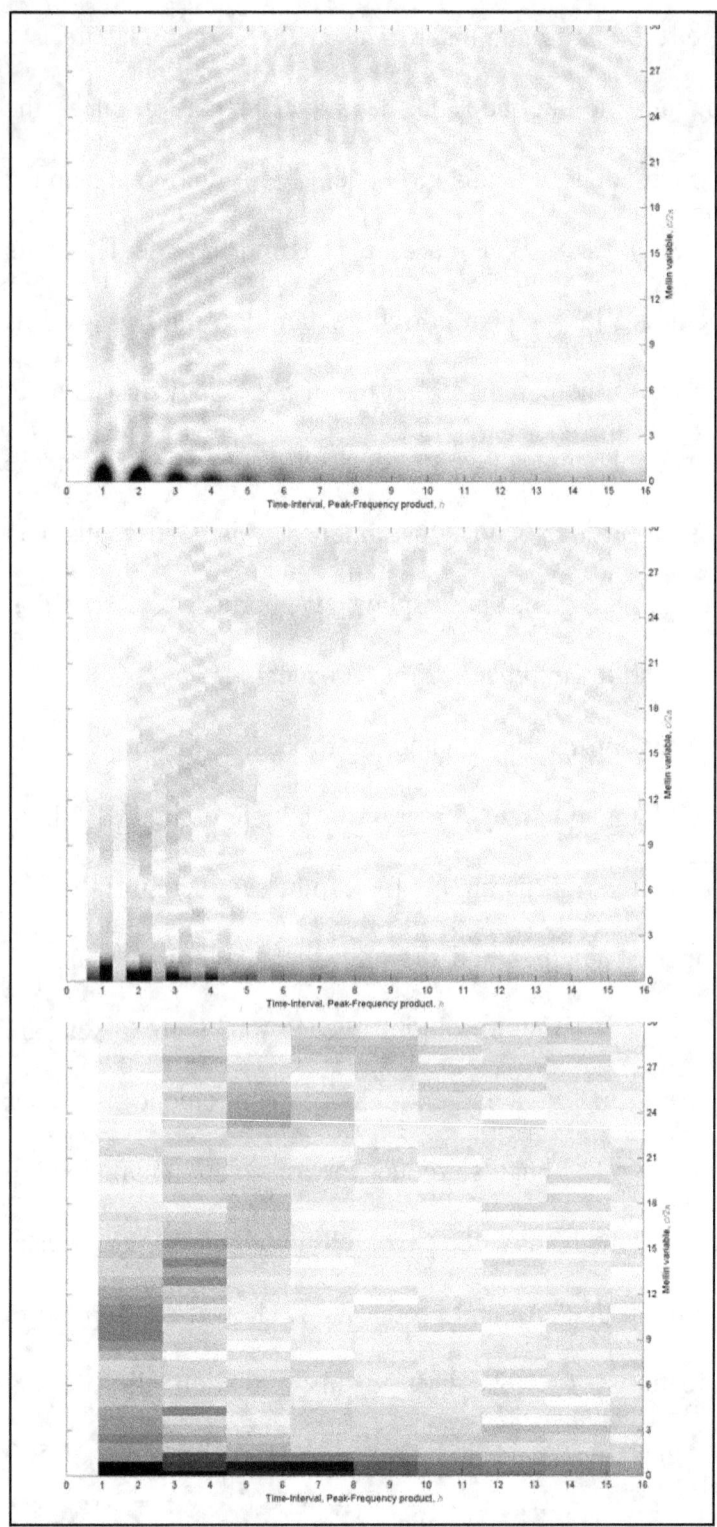

Figure 17. A comparison of the two Mellin image resolutions used in this research compared to the default resolution that aim-mat produces. The top plot is the default *aim-mat* resolution which has about 192,000 features, the middle plot is the one containing 8100 features, and the bottom plot is the one containing 500 features.

34

SAI data was also used to train and test HMM models with HTK; the SAI data used 5600 features.

IV.   Results

Results from each experiment in HTK were output to a master label file (MLF) for analysis by different methods. One method outputs the percent correct recognition of phonemes over the entire test set. Percent correct recognition is defined as $H/N \times 100\%$, where H is the number of correctly identified phonemes and N is the total number of phonemes. The number of correctly identified phonemes is given by: $H = N - S - D$, where D is the number of deletions and S is the number of substitutions. A deletion occurs when a phoneme should have been recognized but was omitted. A substitution occurs when a phoneme is mistaken for a different phoneme. Another output statistic is the percent accuracy defined as $(H - I)/N \times 100\%$, where I is the number of insertions in the output. An insertion occurs when a phoneme is mistakenly inserted into a place where no phoneme should be recognized. Note that the percent accuracy can be negative if enough insertions occur. Most of the results emphasized below are percent correct recognition of phonemes.

4.1 Overall Results

Table 3 shows overall percent correct recognition results from the experiments described in Chapter 3. In this table, the MFCC, MT, and SAI methods and also the

Method	Global Var	# HMM States	# Feat	# Param	Database Sub-set (100 sentences)	Entire Database (6300 sentences)
MFCC	N	3	13	106	40.23%	41.56%
MFCC_D_A	N	3	39	262	50.94%	54.46%
Mellin	N	3	8100	48628	18.85%	14.11%
Mellin	Y	3	8100	48628	20.22%	18.41%
Mellin	N	1	8100	16212	26.23%	23.68%
Mellin	Y	1	8100	16212	30.62%	27.19%
Mellin	N	3	500	3028	16.67%	10.66%
SAI	N	3	4480	26908	N/A	15.55%

Table 3. Comparison of the results of the HTK experiments shown in percent correct recognition. Note that the number of HMM states is the number of emitting states.

varying parameters used in the experiments are compared for percent correct recognition. Since no delta and acceleration coefficients are calculated for the MT data, it is appropriate to compare them to ordinary MFCC results instead of MFCC with delta and acceleration coefficients. This method is included in the table for reference and to observe how the calculation of delta and acceleration coefficients improves percent recognition results. The method column of the table indicates the method of feature extraction: MFCC, MFCC including delta and acceleration coefficients, the MT images at two different resolutions, and finally the SAI image representation. The global variance column indicates whether the initial global variance computed is the same one used throughout all the HMM re-estimations or if the variance for each HMM model is re-estimated during each iteration. The number of HMM states column indicates the number of states used to build the HMM models. As discussed in the previous section, the number of features for the MT data is restricted by HTK to a maximum of 8192; therefore, the maximum number of features used in the MT experiments is 8100. The number of features column indicates how many features each method uses. The number of parameters column indicates the number of parameters that the HMM models must be trained to estimate. The formula for calculating the number of parameters is

$$\# \, parameters = 2 \cdot \left(\# \, states \right) \cdot \left(\# \, features \right) + \left(\# \, states \right) + \left(\# \, states + 2 \right)^{2} \qquad (20)$$

Diagonal covariance matrices were used, so each state must have means and variances equal to the number of features, which is the reason for the factor of two. Adding the number of states is necessary because a global constant is estimated for each state. The final term is a result of the estimation of the state transition matrix. The state transition matrix includes the initial and final state, hence the +2 in this term. The database subset (100 sentences) column shows results in percent correct recognition when a subset of the

TIMIT database is used for training and testing. The final column shows the results in percent correct recognition when the entire TIMIT database is used for training and testing.

The most interesting aspect of the results in Table 3 is the percent correct recognition in each category. The best performing method for MT data recognition is the 1-state HMM with global variances used throughout HMM re-estimations, with a correct recognition rate of 27.2%. It is obvious that the recognition rates are better when the global variances are used in re-estimations than when the variances are re-estimated in each iteration. The reason for this is that the database is not large enough to support accurate training of the individual mixture variances. Also, note that the 1-state models have roughly one-third the number of parameters to estimate compared to the 3-state models. This reduction in the number of parameters for the HMM models to train makes training with the given data faster and produces better performance, but it also yields less flexibility to the models.

Another interesting result is the decrease in performance when the MT data with 500 features is used. The reduction in features results in a reduction in the MT image resolution, which causes a decrease in percent recognition performance. Even though the number of parameters to train is reduced for the MT image with 500 features, the negative effects from a reduced resolution of the MT image outweigh the positive effects of having fewer parameters to train. Since HTK does not accept more than 8192 features, possible performance improvement using more than 8100 features was not explored, but this possibility would be an interesting topic for future research. Also, a lot more data would be required to estimate significantly more parameters.

The SAI data, used in computing the MT data, was also tested and found to perform better than the corresponding case with the MT. This result suggests that some of the parameter settings for the MT and the SAI synchronization component used in this research should be further investigated.

One final observation to take note of from this table is the fact that performance decreases going from the tests on the database subset to tests on the entire database. This result might be due to the properties of the reduced set of speakers, but more research is needed to determine its cause.

A comparison of the MFCC results with the MT and SAI results does show that the MFCCs have better performance, but they have received considerable research and the research on the MT and SAI is just beginning.

4.2 Individual Phoneme Results

To compare performance for individual phonemes, tables 4-6 show the confusion matrices for results from MFCCs (3-state HMMs), MT with 1-state HMMs, and MT with 3-state HMMs, respectively. Both of the MT methods used the global variance during HMM re-estimation. The confusion matrices list all the phonemes in the first column and show a mapping along each row of how each phoneme is recognized in the experiments. The matrices also list the number of insertions and deletions for each phoneme. After the deletions column, the percent correct recognition for each phoneme is listed. The next column lists the broad phonetic class of the phonemes, and the final column gives an average percent correct recognition for each broad phonetic class. Comparison between all three confusion matrices shows an improvement in some, but not all, of the phonemes with the MT method over the MFCC method.

Table 4. Confusion matrix for speech recognition results using MFCCs without delta and acceleration coefficients and 3 state HMMs.

	IY	EY	AE	IH	EH	AH	AX	ER	OW	AA	UH	UW	AO	V	Z	DH	ZH	TH	F	S	HH	CH	JH	N	M	AW	OY	AY	R	L	W	D	B	G	T	P	K	SL	IX	ELR	ENG	EM	Del	% Cor	Avg % Cor
IY	1123	123	13	44	20	19	12	24	18	79	8	24	3	84	44	5	9	10	5	4	13	32	13	19	17	63	3	7	9	7	3	259	26	17	25	40	16	31	7	0	64	59	65	220	45.4	
EY	37	419	9	19	7	4	4	0	4	5	5	4	16	4	6	5	3	1	4	4	28	6	6	5	4	1	0	0	5	9	0	10	4	3	13	9	2	18	3	0	27	8	22	44	59.8	
AE	127	127	865	118	15	47	15	60	11	76	10	39	7	39	12	12	7	5	4	10	88	14	15	11	22	81	8	36	5	4	27	10	3	13	20	12	58	76	8	0	39	34	34	218	43.6	
IH	95	132	26	490	28	60	30	30	44	76	19	62	3	18	40	5	18	15	24	14	67	15	21	55	47	9	9	7	36	12	102	15	27	37	49	14	87	111	14	0	62	56	56	453	22.1	
EH	39	53	69	90	572	19	9	25	30	16	111	75	4	20	50	29	3	25	39	31	39	21	21	11	81	67	26	21	12	26	42	97	33	37	51	29	32	30	53	0	135	30	30	179	34.6	
AH	7	49	60	78	37	156	119	53	94	75	61	16	27	255	29	50	31	2	39	31	72	39	11	81	85	67	71	68	26	26	35	97	33	95	51	29	145	19	53	0	119	30	30	780	16.6		VOWEL
AX	7	17	9	9	0	16	693	5	16	21	6	8	2	34	26	4	1	3	8	10	39	10	10	8	14	5	5	10	10	107	7	7	9	14	18	4	30	10	16	0	6	6	2	118	51.9	
ER	3	9	7	11	2	25	5	290	22	14	4	1	6	19	3	6	2	1	5	5	9	8	8	18	7	28	22	10	107	3	47	7	3	16	5	8	22	25	14	0	14	4	4	96	41.9	
OW	3	11	31	17	4	36	4	9	290	54	1	42	4	40	6	7	2	0	5	9	10	4	8	18	18	78	1	1	1	8	1	47	4	16	5	5	29	14	36	0	14	15	15	163	34.5	
AA	31	13	7	2	2	7	2	11	5	254	4	7	78	17	5	1	3	15	1	9	11	11	8	10	14	3	3	1	3	10	8	8	2	6	8	5	5	2	2	0	5	5	5	46	26.5	
UH	7	6	12	16	8	16	19	1	8	19	14	43	14	43	3	11	3	15	6	14	11	17	17	22	22	1	0	0	4	4	8	8	17	31	11	5	20	37	12	0	32	9	9	195	29.6	
UW	31	10	2	12	13	49	23	2	19	23	8	14	323	18	7	3	7	12	27	5	6	7	4	5	4	37	51	3	2	4	13	101	2	11	20	15	20	9	8	0	9	7	6	459	35.2	
AO	16	5	4	28	2	22	11	4	37	11	4	4	413	70	30	2	2	2	5	27	6	4	2	4	4	5	6	16	5	5	1	13	7	26	11	15	7	2	13	0	12	7	3	65	61.4	32.82%
V	2	4	22	18	1	2	11	0	11	11	16	2	22	56	10	38	14	3	42	23	12	43	3	14	3	5	8	5	3	3	7	4	19	10	11	24	15	16	13	0	25	11	3	50	50.9	
Z	16	5	28	0	3	2	0	0	6	0	25	1	7	56	314	3	19	7	69	196	19	3	5	2	6	6	10	5	5	0	11	1	17	10	0	3	24	3	18	0	3	11	8	179	30.9	
DH	1	1	8	0	3	1	0	0	0	2	0	0	6	9	6	314	1	4	3	1	3	1	5	1	0	8	8	3	0	1	1	3	1	0	5	3	0	0	1	0	3	11	0	31	51.4	
ZH	2	0	3	0	1	1	0	0	2	0	0	0	0	9	15	3	54	0	3	23	0	19	0	2	0	0	10	0	0	1	1	6	0	0	2	5	2	0	0	0	3	1	0	10	70.7	
TH	2	4	2	3	1	0	3	1	1	1	1	0	1	0	2	5	1	515	100	30	3	5	0	4	1	7	7	0	0	1	11	3	2	0	1	2	5	2	1	0	3	0	0	19	65.3		CONSONANT
F	3	5	1	1	1	0	6	5	6	8	1	7	4	17	4	9	2	38	60	769	20	5	5	9	4	4	6	5	3	2	1	6	5	2	4	13	13	16	16	0	16	1	2	113	44.2	
S	7	7	11	8	2	6	9	2	7	3	7	4	2	7	79	18	43	60	26	1700	279	26	6	14	16	3	9	0	9	2	42	1	4	0	0	36	75	41	12	0	8	6	4	119	59.6	
HH	3	9	2	6	4	7	3	9	3	8	5	0	4	1	11	3	6	4	4	5	279	20	43	9	16	1	7	6	4	9	2	2	2	2	0	7	10	3	12	0	0	1	1	16	34.9	
CH	2	1	4	1	0	10	0	0	0	5	0	5	1	1	18	3	12	22	2	7	5	279	6	4	2	0	1	0	0	0	2	5	1	2	8	14	7	22	8	0	5	6	1	15	36.1	
JH	20	25	28	68	12	27	10	10	10	31	18	6	15	25	11	15	1	3	5	13	42	11	28	1	22	30	1	1	18	9	29	38	40	91	42	65	66	33	34	0	43	36	32	395	56.9	
N	3	14	13	9	0	12	2	0	2	17	6	7	39	39	27	1	9	40	35	5	16	38	12	90	60	10	5	7	4	2	8	18	17	84	21	20	20	33	8	0	2	41	3	122	36.1	
AW	0	9	1	8	2	5	5	7	8	2	7	4	6	6	2	2	2	0	0	0	1	2	3	0	1	106	2	7	2	2	2	2	1	2	2	7	7	2	5	0	5	2	0	22	49.3		diphthong
OY	5	22	2	6	4	9	14	4	2	11	5	15	8	15	0	1	4	0	1	1	2	2	4	3	18	5	149	19	11	2	16	5	5	7	2	11	2	2	8	0	12	8	2	14	53.6	
AY	12	35	21	26	9	13	11	9	11	16	23	57	7	66	18	4	18	36	7	19	26	26	38	21	37	19	489	32	11	6	54	5	7	14	50	78	11	30	10	0	10	10	2	55	57.9		semivowel
R	20	40	48	21	7	12	12	5	0	28	65	13	63	18	9	9	2	12	14	7	16	16	26	28	53	33	119	32	1115	1111	200	54	27	53	5	46	46	3	224	0	32	10	5	436	37.9	
L	29	10	6	5	4	4	4	1	1	4	4	2	1	21	0	1	1	7	1	9	5	5	5	5	5	0	0	3	16	4	6	6	0	6	5	6	6	3	6	0	10	7	1	282	45.1	
W	0	0	0	0	3	0	0	2	0	15	18	33	0	66	11	11	8	20	17	12	22	59	26	73	33	13	27	11	6	18	534	6	22	188	48	33	10	22	9	0	37	25	1	66	74	
D	14	46	15	49	16	17	17	8	5	24	5	18	11	9	46	46	3	20	17	22	59	26	6	1	58	4	11	4	11	6	2	14	443	618	33	137	98	22	4	0	4	25	5	344	23.8	
B	8	8	9	11	16	9	4	2	2	30	11	5	18	42	30	30	1	6	20	12	30	1	16	11	11	11	3	4	3	6	6	6	12	54	59	29	98	33	4	0	5	5	6	101	69.4		consonant stop
G	8	10	9	44	3	12	4	3	6	41	8	28	10	42	58	58	1	63	2	68	30	3	93	1	49	22	4	3	30	30	22	18	8	82	59	399	29	33	4	0	5	17	5	62	41.9	
T	29	40	27	79	33	24	30	32	17	9	4	6	1	10	30	30	8	40	36	17	131	38	35	49	22	0	57	32	6	6	9	19	19	59	52	433	399	92	43	0	81	36	4	683	12.2	
P	14	25	25	12	2	0	5	0	0	5	8	4	6	8	26	26	0	36	17	17	5	5	12	12	8	8	4	4	6	6	10	10	14	35	52	433	433	761	15	0	7	17	5	24	84.8	
K	0	0	0	0	0	0	0	0	0	0	0	0	0	0	2	2	0	0	0	0	0	0	0	0	8	0	0	0	0	0	0	0	0	0	0	0	0	0	0	0	11	17	5	189	38.6	
SIL	0	0	0	0	0	0	0	0	0	0	0	0	0	0	0	0	0	0	0	0	0	0	0	0	0	0	0	0	0	0	0	0	0	0	0	0	0	3360	0	0	0	0	0	1	33.3	
IX	175	363	171	388	354	364	188	185	227	166	123	291	160	193	105	246	108	216	244	345	167	428	137	110	226	286	180	188	185	133	305	227	188	298	52	37	52	361	298	88	184	268	37	0	57.5	
Sum	1544	1281	1329	1245	1216	1210	1680	1007	732	649	1771	295	982	862	1185	2224	687	437	1584	1720	686	784	953	1370	1347	1749	1690	977	3042	1206	3360	1044	820	899	174	49	37						6426		36.12%

40

Table 5. Confusion matrix for speech recognition results using MT data and 1-state HMMs.

Table 6. Confusion matrix for speech recognition results using MT data and 3-state HMMs.

	IY	EY	AE	IH	EH	AH	AX	ER	OW	AA	UH	UW	AO	V	Z	DH	ZH	SH	TH	F	S	HH	CH	JH	N	M	AW	OY	AY	R	L	Y	W	D	B	G	TP	K	SIL	EL	AXR	NG	EN	EM	Del	% Cor		Avg % Cor
IY	678	57	17	32	0	4	10	8	24	10	31	81	9	66	3	16	11	7	3	28	82	117	2	37	22	29	86	5	10	1	2	6	0	17	8	183	8	0	0	0	0	1	0	0	1001	40.1	VOWEL	
EY	14	174	20	20	4	0	7	7	6	8	24	24	6	22	0	3	11	0	0	10	10	21	10	21	19	16	32	3	1	0	0	0	0	0	0	50	8	0	0	0	0	0	0	1	296	37.7		
AE	22	36	739	25	0	2	5	1	15	2	53	53	8	57	4	0	17	8	4	34	28	34	28	5	33	45	90	0	15	0	0	0	0	0	16	152	8	2	0	0	0	0	0	0	778	51.8		
IH	55	46	58	1	0	3	12	0	8	5	21	95	0	93	5	5	39	13	34	80	62	34	39	14	35	24	133	0	19	0	0	0	0	0	18	181	16	2	0	0	0	0	0	0	1531	0.1		
EH	13	15	46	0	1	0	7	1	7	0	10	40	0	46	0	8	13	5	20	34	29	80	62	12	11	34	67	0	30	0	0	0	0	1	5	64	13	0	0	0	0	0	0	0	601	17.6		
AH	59	66	69	112	0	0	28	0	34	7	10	173	0	168	8	18	62	13	20	122	132	40	115	44	11	115	233	0	30	0	0	1	5	0	24	303	25	6	0	0	0	0	0	0	2267	2		
AX	0	0	0	0	0	0	0	0	0	0	0	0	0	0	0	0	0	0	0	0	0	0	0	0	0	0	0	0	0	0	0	0	0	0	0	1	0	0	0	0	0	0	0	0	0	0		
ER	11	7	28	31	0	7	0	0	1	1	11	64	1	49	3	7	15	3	3	32	48	4	21	6	52	33	110	0	12	0	1	2	3	3	13	128	7	2	0	0	0	1	0	0	730	8.6		
OW	9	12	14	0	0	1	7	0	62	0	5	18	0	24	2	1	20	2	1	17	13	13	14	4	6	52	49	0	9	0	0	1	0	1	6	100	5	1	0	0	0	0	0	0	365	21.3		
AA	3	3	28	0	0	0	0	0	1	240	11	38	0	39	0	0	38	0	0	38	17	38	17	2	14	6	79	0	0	0	0	0	0	0	2	10	7	0	0	0	0	0	0	0	634	32		
UH	12	15	0	0	0	0	4	0	0	0	75	28	0	8	0	0	4	0	0	10	2	5	5	2	5	3	13	0	0	0	0	0	0	0	2	10	5	1	0	0	0	0	0	0	67	53.2		
UW	19	26	39	6	0	6	8	0	2	2	28	37	180	32	1	0	10	6	0	25	34	20	3	5	22	17	76	34	8	0	0	0	0	2	0	88	6	0	0	0	0	0	0	0	483	32		
AO	13	6	6	3	0	0	1	0	8	0	25	37	25	44	1	1	5	1	2	10	5	15	5	2	27	5	22	0	2	0	0	0	0	0	7	131	4	2	0	0	0	0	0	0	730	5.3	22.96%	
V	13	33	1	5	0	3	2	0	16	1	63	7	16	301	0	2	55	0	0	6	6	5	41	1	17	4	79	1	2	0	0	0	0	0	2	37	4	2	0	0	0	0	0	0	262	63.2	CONSONANT	
Z	10	18	0	0	0	0	7	0	0	0	38	11	0	42	18	31	8	0	23	7	19	81	0	28	18	8	75	0	0	0	3	0	0	3	12	91	3	3	0	0	0	0	0	0	653	2.3		
DH	10	18	0	0	0	2	0	0	0	0	3	38	0	17	0	0	5	6	20	4	7	150	0	4	18	7	4	0	0	0	1	0	0	0	4	107	3	3	0	0	0	0	0	0	661	5.8		
ZH	4	14	0	0	0	0	2	0	2	0	10	3	0	2	0	0	2	0	0	3	9	3	0	1	6	7	21	0	0	0	0	1	0	0	0	29	4	0	0	0	0	0	0	0	36	12.5		
SH	3	2	0	0	0	6	6	0	0	0	9	8	0	17	0	1	6	9	2	3	7	9	0	0	11	4	11	0	1	0	0	0	1	1	2	20	2	0	0	0	0	0	0	0	403	3.9		
TH	7	14	4	0	0	0	4	0	0	0	58	60	3	50	0	0	21	3	8	6	41	25	2	3	18	6	52	0	5	0	5	0	0	0	1	75	3	6	0	0	0	0	0	0	105	4.5		
F	5	14	0	4	0	4	2	0	5	0	16	17	0	12	1	3	21	22	0	0	1216	28	89	9	17	18	79	1	11	0	10	0	0	0	0	127	3	6	0	0	0	0	0	0	489	5.1		
S	29	0	0	0	0	6	2	0	3	0	17	6	3	12	1	1	9	9	5	1	1	209	34	0	4	8	27	0	0	0	0	0	0	0	10	35	5	6	0	0	0	2	0	0	753	64.3		
HH	2	8	0	0	0	2	2	0	1	0	6	6	0	11	1	0	3	2	4	1	4	5	9	2	5	11	15	1	1	0	0	2	2	0	4	18	2	0	0	0	1	0	0	0	301	46.5		
CH	5	0	0	0	0	2	1	0	0	0	12	4	0	11	1	0	10	0	1	2	5	18	5	7	3	4	5	2	22	0	1	1	4	0	2	29	2	1	0	0	0	1	0	0	91	66.1		
JH	34	14	6	19	0	5	2	0	8	1	22	32	4	92	8	8	40	3	4	6	56	56	2	5	7	39	145	0	9	0	9	1	0	1	19	245	18	1	0	0	0	2	0	1	128	4.1		
N	25	0	3	12	0	2	2	0	1	0	106	15	12	59	7	7	17	2	0	2	25	42	2	0	6	21	102	1	0	0	2	1	4	1	4	132	10	0	0	0	2	3	1	1	1310	39.5		
M	2	0	3	15	0	3	1	0	17	0	7	4	7	3	0	0	17	3	0	2	25	25	0	0	743	265	10	0	0	0	2	0	0	0	0	23	1	0	0	0	0	3	2	2	660	28.5		
AW	1	3	0	1	0	2	0	0	3	0	4	12	0	0	0	4	0	3	5	2	1	2	2	2	3	1	214	0	0	0	0	1	0	0	0	7	0	7	0	0	0	0	0	0	46	87	diphthong	35.98%
OY	0	3	0	0	0	0	5	0	1	0	33	2	0	39	0	0	18	0	3	0	15	21	2	1	23	8	60	12	10	0	0	0	6	0	0	58	0	10	0	0	0	0	0	0	446	2.6		35.70%
AY	19	13	31	13	0	8	13	0	11	0	78	56	0	136	11	30	43	7	22	4	99	46	20	63	83	231	11	16	0	8	16	0	5	5	28	261	16	3	0	0	1	3	0	1	1420	28.8		
R	21	26	13	22	0	6	8	0	30	0	115	18	5	118	7	11	37	5	5	24	84	40	36	17	2	29	195	3	17	6	6	11	0	1	25	198	8	6	0	0	1	2	2	0	1472	1.2	semivowel	
L	23	14	42	4	0	0	0	0	10	0	20	14	4	22	0	7	11	8	10	4	40	24	4	6	9	17	42	0	0	1	3	3	2	1	6	62	4	2	0	0	0	0	0	0	433	3.1		
Y	22	17	8	10	0	5	9	0	31	0	89	15	0	38	2	3	27	10	4	2	49	46	24	6	29	18	83	3	12	2	3	3	3	28	10	224	9	2	0	0	0	0	0	1	720	5.5		15.00%
W	22	17	0	6	0	0	0	0	6	0	21	30	1	39	0	15	2	2	7	10	14	16	14	2	10	8	44	0	5	0	0	1	3	1	0	113	0	3	0	0	1	2	1	1	1238	2.9		
D	10	7	6	2	0	2	3	0	3	0	33	12	21	30	5	0	13	2	2	4	14	16	6	6	2	14	36	4	0	5	2	0	0	0	13	113	6	1	0	0	1	1	1	0	505	22	consonant stop	
B	5	7	14	3	0	3	1	0	5	0	12	22	1	96	6	6	34	13	15	4	80	147	2	3	50	39	145	1	18	0	5	1	3	0	0	365	6	6	0	0	1	8	1	4	430	17.7		
T	34	46	60	19	0	6	2	0	19	0	113	35	21	8	3	27	30	30	67	0	67	0	0	0	55	45	84	3	12	4	12	0	4	3	16	292	6	4	0	0	0	1	0	2	1900	90.4		
P	25	22	26	16	0	0	0	0	0	0	87	18	0	71	3	2	0	0	0	0	0	0	0	0	0	0	0	0	0	0	0	0	0	0	0	809	6	46	0	0	0	0	1	1	195	4.4		19.45%
K	0	0	0	0	0	0	0	0	0	0	0	0	0	0	0	0	0	0	0	0	0	0	0	0	0	0	0	0	0	0	0	0	0	0	0	0	0	0	3360	0	0	0	0	0	1088	0		
SIL	0	0	0	0	0	0	0	0	0	0	0	0	0	0	0	0	0	0	0	0	0	0	0	0	0	0	0	0	0	0	0	0	0	0	0	0	0	0	0	0	0	0	0	0	0	0		
IX	0	0	0	0	0	0	0	0	0	0	0	0	0	0	0	0	0	0	1	0	0	0	0	0	0	0	0	0	0	0	0	0	0	0	0	0	0	0	0	0	0	0	0	0	2	0		
EL	0	0	0	0	0	0	0	0	0	0	0	0	0	0	0	0	0	0	0	0	0	0	0	0	0	0	0	0	0	0	0	0	0	0	0	0	0	0	0	0	0	0	0	0	0	0		
AXR	1	4	0	3	0	0	2	3	2	2	15	5	5	7	1	3	3	1	3	3	0	7	11	7	11	5	20	5	1	0	0	5	5	2	21	33	0	2	0	0	1	1	1	1	199	5.5		
NG	0	0	0	0	0	0	0	0	0	0	0	0	0	0	0	0	0	0	0	0	0	0	0	0	0	0	0	0	0	0	0	0	0	0	0	0	0	0	0	0	0	0	0	0	0	0.5		
EN																																																
EM																																																
Sum	1189	802	1635	442	68	170	330	689	1869	624	112	2007	132	187	98	94	145	1884	1302	1834	118	1452	713	1322	2916	847	30	65	132	67	452	323	5042	118	3360	1	33	36	21	0						25504	0		
Ins	46	76	79	40	6	2	17	39	150	32	6	238	7	5	10	10	8	55	92	170	8	77	40	108	207	29	2	2	6	20	21	20	268	6	1	0	0	4	0	0						0			

Table 7 lists the phonemes with improved percent correct recognition performance using the MT features with either 1-state HMMs or 3-state HMMs over the MFCC features (without delta and acceleration coefficients). Each of the MT methods used the global variance for all re-estimations. Both the percent correct recognition rates and the percent accuracy rates are shown for each type of feature set. In some cases the accuracy percentage was negative. Obviously, the MT data does not perform equally well in all 1-state and 3-state cases. Even though the MT features did not outperform the MFCCs overall, improvement was found for some phonemes. The increase in performance found for these phonemes with the MT might be exploited by fusing the particular phoneme models that have improved performance for the MT with existing models of HMMs trained with MFCCs. Also, it is important to note that the MFCCs

Phoneme	MFCC		Mellin-1 State		Mellin-3 State	
	% Cor	% Acc	% Cor	% Acc	% Cor	% Acc
IY	45.41%	38.33%	56.07%	-284.49%	40.07%	37.35%
AE	43.55%	34.94%	13.32%	-601.05%	51.82%	46.28%
OW	41.91%	14.02%	55.08%	-48.57%	21.28%	17.26%
AA	5.01%	-14.06%	38.36%	-3846.17%	32.00%	26.80%
UH	26.54%	-153.09%	52.94%	-149.02%	53.19%	-53.19%
UW	29.85%	15.39%	54.48%	-178.65%	31.97%	26.29%
V	61.37%	-18.13%	11.62%	-411.48%	63.24%	13.24%
DH	30.88%	6.69%	39.95%	-114.64%	5.79%	4.49%
HH	44.22%	-23.61%	56.99%	-4376.16%	46.55%	26.06%
CH	59.61%	5.88%	79.09%	-2321.29%	66.11%	-28.33%
N	36.09%	25.90%	10.62%	9.64%	39.48%	35.39%
M	56.88%	41.49%	75.91%	17.27%	28.49%	24.19%
AW	49.30%	-824.41%	68.10%	-17515.95%	50.31%	-16.77%
OY	53.60%	-11.15%	87.89%	-1912.80%	86.99%	2.85%
D	23.80%	11.61%	27.66%	-6.12%	2.90%	2.90%
P	84.80%	79.92%	83.08%	-134.77%	90.39%	60.45%
K	38.59%	20.28%	54.75%	-87.40%	4.37%	3.80%

Table 7. The results of the HTK recognition process for phonemes with improved recognition performance using MT features over MFCC features.

have been finely tuned over decades of research, while the MT features are just starting to be investigated, and thus further research on the MT features may yield better results.

V.   Discussion and Recommendations

Research previously conducted on vowel recognition using the MT [11] [17] suggested the possibility of improved speech recognition results with MT features. This previous research used a Mixture of Gaussians model on single simulated vowel frames to perform vowel recognition [3] [11]. Since all broad phonetic classes of real speech were used in this research, not just synthetic vowels, it is more general than previous research.

This research reported here differs from this previous research in that it uses HMMs to conduct the phoneme recognition experiments. Since the HMMs are based on having synchronous feature vectors, adding the extra step of SAI synchronization was necessary. This step, while converting the SAI to synchronous form, might have contributed to a decrease in recognition performance results due to some of the design choices made. Investigating the tradeoff of some of these design choices related to synchronization may lead to better recognition performance. Alternatively, a method of speech recognition that does not require synchronous data (thus enabling the SAI to remain asynchronous) may produce better results.

There are a number of variations to try in future research. One variation to try is feature normalization. The MT features were not normalized to take into account overall magnitude differences between frames utterances. Feature mean and variance normalization, for example, may improve results. Another variation to try is using more than one mixture for each state in the HMM models. This would make the models more complicated but might make them more discriminating, thereby leading to improved results. Also, changing the algorithms used to calculate the various components of the

AIM to more complex ones may yield a tradeoff of computational complexity for improved results.

Rather than increasing the complexity of the recognition system, methods that reduce the complexity of the system but that retain as much information as possible in the data may be beneficial. For instance, principal components analysis (PCA) is a linear transformation that reduces the dimensionality of a dataset while retaining as much of the information as possible contained in the dataset. Another possible method for reducing complexity is to use marginal distributions (*e.g.*, temporal and spectral profiles), of the image data, where feature vectors that sum down the rows and across the columns of the data matrix are employed. Figure 18 shows an example of the marginal distributions of a SAI image frame. Similar processing could be done with the MT images. While PCA and marginal distributions might reduce feature information, they also might allow better trained HMMs given the small amount of data available in the TIMIT database.

As shown in the results section, some phonemes did increase in correct recognition performance when MT features were used instead of MFCC features. It may be beneficial to attempt fusion of the phoneme models trained with MT data that show improvement with existing MFCC-based models that perform relatively well.

In summary, using the MT features lead to improved phoneme recognition rates for some phonemes. The results obtained here further the AFRL/HECP mission in improving human-machine collaboration, and future research should be able to use these results to explore ways to further improve speech recognition.

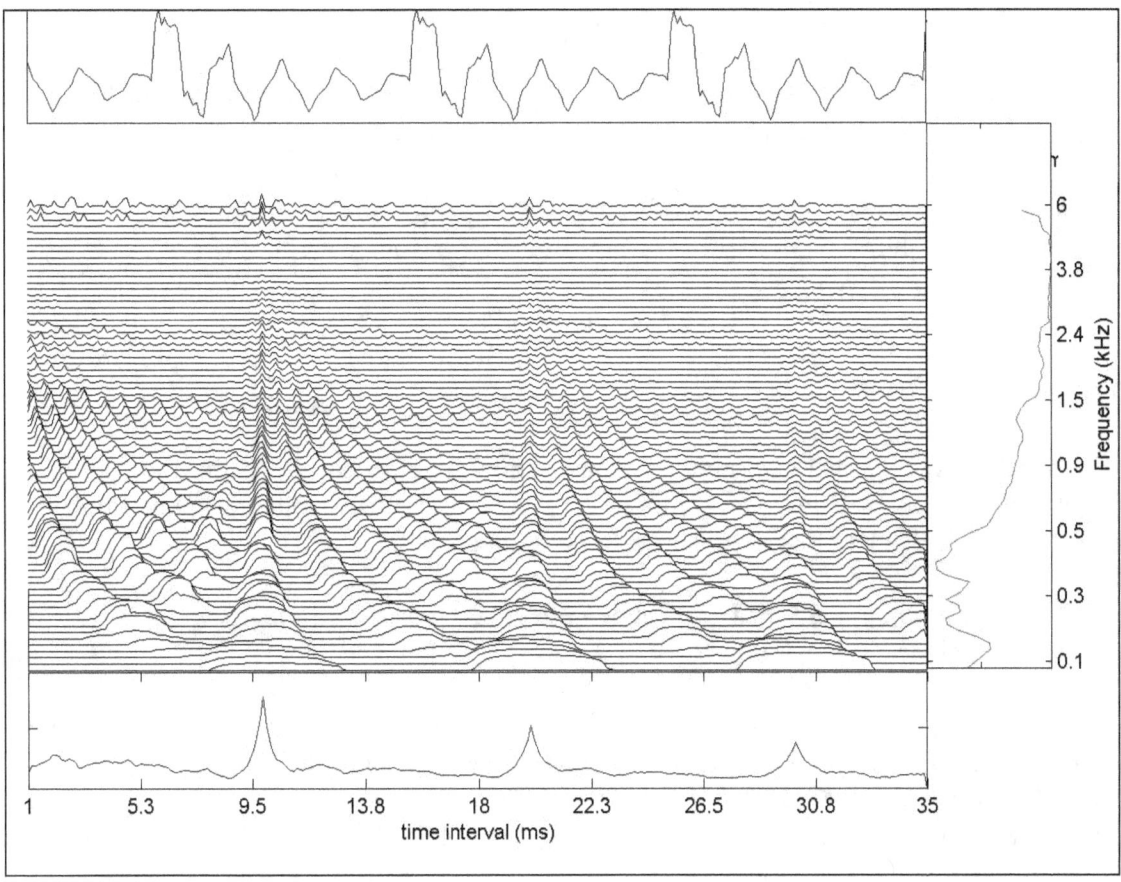

Figure 18. Marginal distributions of a SAI frame. The waveform at the top of the figure is the original speech waveform. The waveform at the bottom is the temporal profile of the SAI image, which is obtained by summing down the columns of the SAI data matrix. The waveform on the right is the spectral profile of the SAI image, which is obtained by summing across the rows of the SAI data matrix.

Bibliography

1. Rabiner, Lawrence and Biing-Hwang Juang. *Fundamentals of Speech Recognition*, pp. 1,339-340, PTR Prentice-Hall, Inc., (Engelwood, NJ), 1993.

2. Weisstein, Eric W. "Mellin Transform." From *MathWorld*--A Wolfram Web Resource, 2006. http://mathworld.wolfram.com/MellinTransform.html

3. Turner, Richard E., Marc Al-Hames, and Roy Patterson. "Vowel Recognition using the Mellin Image." Centre of the Neural Basis of Hearing, Dept of Physiology, University of Cambridge, 2003.

4. Young, Steve, Gunnar Evermann, Thomas Hain, Dan Kershaw, Gareth Moore, Julian Odell, Dave Ollason, Dan Povey, Valtcho Valtchev, and Phil Woodland. "The HTK Book." Cambridge University, (Cambridge, England). 2002.

5. Duda, Richard O., Peter E. Hart, David G. Stork. *Pattern Classification*, pp. 128-138, Wiley-Interscience, (New York, NY), 2001.

6. Kamm, Terri, Hynek Hermansky, and Andreas G. Andreou. "Learning the Mel-scale and Optimal VTN Mapping." Johns Hopkins University, Center for Language and Speech Processing, 1997 workshop (WS97), 1997. http://www.clsp.jhu.edu/ws97/acoustic/reports/KHAMel.pdf

7. Bleeck, Stefan, and Roy Patterson. "*Aim-mat*: An implementation of the auditory image model in MATLAB." 2004. http://www.mrc-cbu.cam.ac.uk/cnbh/aimmanual/Introduction/Introductionframeset.htm

8. Turner, Richard E., Marc A. Al-Hames, David R. R. Smith, Hideki Kawahara, Toshio Irino, and Roy D. Patterson. "Vowel normalization: Time-domain processing of the internal dynamics of speech." in *Dynamics of Speech Production and Perception*, ed. P. Divenyi, IOS Press, (Amsterdam, The Netherlands), (in press.)

9. Anderson, Timothy R. "A comparison of auditory models for speaker independent phoneme recognition", IEEE International Conference on Acoustics Speech and Signal Processing, p. 231, 1993.

10. Patterson, Roy D. "Auditory images: How complex sounds are represented in the auditory system," *Journal of the Acoustical Society of America*, vol. 21, pp. 183-190, 2000.

11. Irino, Toshio and Roy Patterson. "Segregating information about the size and shape of the vocal tract using a time-domain auditory model: The stabilized wavelet-Mellin transform." *Speech Communication*, vol. 36, no 3, pp. 181-203, March 2002.

12. Tung, Y.K. "Uncertainty on Travel Time in Kinematic Wave Channel Routing." Channel Flow and Catchment Runoff Proceedings of the International Conference for Centennial of Manning's Formula and Kuichling's Rational Formula, Wyoming Water Research Center and Statistics Department, University of Wyoming, 1989. http://library.wrds.uwyo.edu/wrp/89-30/89-30.html

13. Guo, Xiaoxin, Zhiwen Xu, Yinan Lu, and Yunjie Pang. "An Application of Fourier-Mellin Transform in Image Registration," The Fifth International Conference on Computer and Information Technology (CIT'05), Shanghai, China, pp. 619-623, 2005.

14. De Sena, Antonio and Davide Rocchesso. "A Fast Mellin Transform with Applications in DAFx," Proc. Of the 7th Int. Conference on Digital Audio Effects (DAFx'04), (Naples, Italy), pp. 65-66, October 5-8, 2004.

15. Cambridge University Engineering Department, Microsoft Corporation. Hidden Markov Model Toolkit. http://htk.eng.cam.ac.uk, December 2002.

16. Garofolo, J.S., L.F. Lamel, W.M. Fisher, J.G. Fiscus, D.S. Pallett, and N.L. Dahlgren. "readme.doc," p1, The DARPA TIMIT Acoustic-Phonetic Continuous Speech Corpus (TIMIT), Training and Test Data, NIST Speech Disc CD1-1.1, 1993.

17. Turner, Richard E. "The Perception of Scale in Speech: Vowel Recognition and the Mellin Transform, Part III Project" pp. 4-5, 2003. http://www.mrc-cbu.cam.ac.uk/~tw01/cnbh/teaching/physics_project/documents/PartIII2003.pdf

18. Brookes, Mike. VOICEBOX: Speech Processing Toolbox for MATLAB. Imperial College of Science, Technology, and Medicine, University of London, Oct 2005. http://www.ee.ic.ac.uk/hp/staff/dmb/voicebox/voicebox.html